Maria Brand

From the Land of Westphalia to the Shores of the Pacific

Maria Brand

authorHOUSE®

AuthorHouse™
1663 Liberty Drive
Bloomington, IN 47403
www.authorhouse.com
Phone: 1-800-839-8640

© 2010 Maria Brand. All rights reserved.

No part of this book may be reproduced, stored in a retrieval system, or transmitted by any means without the written permission of the author.

First published by AuthorHouse 5/20/2010

ISBN: 978-1-4520-1395-4 (e)
ISBN: 978-1-4520-1396-1 (sc)

Library of Congress Control Number: 2010906311

Printed in the United States of America
Bloomington, Indiana

This book is printed on acid-free paper.

The bonnet Maria Brand is wearing is part of a Westphalian native dress still worn in the 1950s. Maria would wear it at the many German American exhibits she and her husband presented in the San Francisco Bay Area.

About The Book

I believe many immigrants can identify with this book, because we all share the experience of being uprooted, having to learn a new language and losing our children to a culture we can never fully embrace. This, we all share, regardless of what continent we call home.

In addition, if you come from a country that America is or has been at war with, it is difficult to endure the constant propaganda against your country of origin, where many of your relatives may still reside. I have written about the pain I felt every time I heard the word "Nazi" applied to all of my people.

To relieve my frustration, I tried to document the way I grew up in the West Muensterland, near the Dutch border, how I met and married my husband in Hawaii, and our life together including raising our two sons. I have written about our successes and failures, our anxieties and joys, and growing old together.

I have included letters to senators and congressmen regarding current issues and their replies. You will also read how my husband and I promoted the contributions Germans in America have made for more than 350 years.

For all this effort, we where honored by the "German American Heritage Foundation of the USA" in 2003, as well as by the German Government in the year 2000.

I lost my partner and best friend of 45 years in 2005.

I continue my efforts and research via the internet. My web-site is listed on the back cover of the book.

I am grateful to America for broadening my horizons and opening paths I would not have dared to walk on in Germany. I also believe America was blessed by having so many Germans come to these shores.

Maria Brand

Memories by Maria Brand

In memory of my parents, my husband, Walter and for our sons, Ralph and Raymond, their wives Caroline and Barbara, respectively, and our grandsons, Christopher, Richard, and Gerard.

Contents

About The Book vii
Memories by Maria Brand ix
My early childhood 1
In 1939, World War II started 5
The war begins to have an impact on our lives 11
1948: The situation begins to improve 20
I graduated from school in 1950 and worked in different places 21
Leaving home to come to America 26
Starting life in Milwaukee in 1956 30
My journey to Hawaii and my early beginnings there 35
Biographical sketch of Walter Brand, my husband 39
Honolulu, where our lives together started 46
Ralph, our oldest son, was born November 12, 1961 51
First trip to Germany; my father died 55
We bought our first property, a duplex, May 1, 1964 58
Second trip to Germany; Walter's father died 60
Raymond entered our small family 62
In 1966 we bought the duplex on Twenty-sixth Avenue 65
Moving to Sunnyvale in 1968 68
Boys' school years—hard on them, hard on me 70
Our friends in San Francisco 75
Joining the Germania Verein in San Jose 76
Walter suffered a heart attack on August 8, 1977 78
Ralph joined the air force 80
Wedding in St. Neots; life in California and back to England 82
Ray: high school years, air force, San Jose State, marriage 84
Bed and breakfast business 88

Flower business 90
A rough awakening: learning about the world and its hypocrisies 91
The New York press, 1911; nothing has changed 98
Researching German-American history 100
Walter passes away unexpectedly 102
Starting a Web site..104
Moving to The Villages, a retirement community..........................105
Have I ever regretted coming to America? 110
A week in Berchtesgaden..112
New Year's Eve..118
Karneval, the last hurrah before Lent...119
Has Karneval changed over the years?..120
Palm Sunday is especially for small children 122
Easter celebration as I remember it...124
Springtime is for planting...127
May is the month of Mary 128
Labor Day, first of May 129
Pentecost, Pfingsten, Pfingstbraut...130
Schuetzenfest..131
Farmer's wedding in Westphalia...133
A new baby in the family..137
Kaffeeklatsch 138
Wo man singt da lass dich nieder, boese Menschen ken-
   nen keine Lieder Where people sing, it's safe to settle 139
Assumption of Mary, August 16, apple procession........................141
August: harvesting the grain fields 142
Richtfest, raising the roof 143
Harvesting the potatoes..144
Kirchweih: consecration of the church...146
Stomping the sauerkraut...148
Oktoberfest in Bavaria..150
All Saints Day and All Souls Day...152
Praying for the departed 155
Schlachttag, or slaughter day 156
Schlachtfest, or slaughter feast 158
St. Nick as I remember it..159

Christmas as I remember it 163
Tribute to the German mothers and grandmothers of
  World War II 167
Hans and Trudy's golden anniversary 170
We must know our homeland in order to love it 175
Purpose of Exhibit 177
The German Hausfrau, an endangered species? 179
Letter to Richard, my second grandson 183
Pacific Singing Society visits Philadelphia 185
An appeal to the German American community 190
Can a Muslim be a good American? 194
My reply 196
Another subject I like to mention is gay marriage 198
On taking Christ out of Christmas 199
My response 201
On immigration 203
Letter to the editor and my reply 208
Letters and responses to and from people in Government
  and others 212
Recipients of the Distinguished German American of the
  Year Award 239

xiii

My early childhood

I was born on March 30, 1936, in a small town called Vreden, Germany. This city is located in the West-Muensterland near the Dutch border. After the Second World War, all the surrounding townships were incorporated. Vreden can now boast a population of about twenty thousand. This city is ancient, as the documents in Xanthene's archives prove. Vreden was mentioned as early as 839 AD, which was during Charlemagne's reign. In the nineteenth century the city was burned to the ground twice and was rebuilt, to be destroyed again by the Allied bombings on March 21, 1945.

I was the fifth of six children, consisting of two boys and four girls. We lived in a duplex on the outskirts of town. My father's brother and his family lived in one half of the building and we lived in the other half.

The first memory I have is of the day my younger sister was born. I was a little more than three years old. I remember I was standing on a chair in the kitchen. Someone, (I don't know who), was helping me get dressed when I was told we had a new little sister. This was on June 13, 1939, the feast day of St Anthony. My father's brother was going to be the godfather, and since his name was Anton, it was decided rather quickly that my sister's name was going to be Antonia, which is feminine for Anton.

Our house was spacious, but only the kitchen and a small room next to it could be heated. Most activities took place in the kitchen— the cooking, eating, bathing on Saturday, canning in the summer, and sausage making in the winter, when a pig was butchered. In the winter, on laundry days, the frozen sheets, etc., were taken off the line and brought into the kitchen and hung over chairs for the warm air to dry them before they found their way back in the Schrank (cabinets). The kitchen was our play and study room as well. In the winter evenings, we often sat around the wood-burning stove knitting or mending socks while at the same time we sang every song that came to mind. We took turns sticking our feet into the baking tube to keep them warm, or we placed them on a wooden footstool, which served as a foot warmer.

I have seen this footstool only in our region and a couple of times in an old Dutch painting. The foot warmer was a square cube made of wood; it had slats on top. Three sides were enclosed; the fourth side had a door that covered the lower half of the opening and could be moved up and down. This door was used to secure a small iron bucket, filled with glowing coal and placed inside the box. It gave comforting warmth to the user.

If we were not singing, we sat around the kitchen table playing a board game called "Mensch aergere dich nicht," (Aggravation). This kept us occupied for long periods of time and helped mom keep her sanity. I still like to sing and know many songs by heart. Often our cousins from next door came over and joined in. Sometimes, as a treat, we had apples baking in the oven. The fragrance would fill the kitchen.

We had three bedrooms. The parents' bedroom had two large beds; the others had one. My older sisters, Gertrud and Lissi, slept together, and so did my brothers, Jup and Hermann. Toni and I shared a bed in the parents' bedroom; eight people, four large beds. A brick was kept in the baking tube of the wood-burning stove during the day and, wrapped in a towel at bedtime, served as a bed warmer when needed.

The bed also served as a food warmer. Leftovers from the main meal at noon (usually a one-pot meal) were scooped into a bowl, which then had a lid placed on top of it and a towel wrapped around it. It was then placed in between the bedcovers. The food would keep warm until supper time, when it appeared and was served alongside pancakes or some kind of cream soup, in which we crumbled pumpernickel. In the Muensterland region the menu was simple—meat or Speck (bacon), lots of vegetables and potatoes, all placed in one pot and boiled. Pancakes of all kinds, including potato pancakes, were another staple in our diet along with an assortment of soups, such as fruit soups, vegetable soup, or cream soups, which all tasted so good. My mother was an excellent soup chef.

In the afternoon we would sometimes have a sandwich. It was always either rye bread or pumpernickel; butter was used sparingly, and so were the cold cuts. A prayer was said before and after every meal. All this was good and healthy and common in our area. We never felt deprived of anything.

Our upstairs was rented out to a family from Holland. They lived there with four adults, used our toilet, and had a piece of our garden to plant their own vegetables. They often were downstairs as if they were part of the family, and I always thought they were. The arrangement was beneficial to both families. They helped each other whenever help was needed.

In the evening, especially in the winter months, it was dark at four thirty in the afternoon. The pigs needed to be fed. They were kept in a little brick house about twenty yards from the house, which we called "Schoepken." The pigsty was separated from the storage area where we and our renters stored the bikes and also the feed for the pigs, chickens, and rabbits. The smaller animals were kept in the back of the Schoepken. There was no electricity. A lantern was lit, and one of us children had to hold it while mom or dad fed the pigs. On laundry day the bikes were moved outside, and the storage area became the laundry room. The day before wash day the laundry was sorted and placed in big tubs to soak. Water was hauled from the house and heated in a huge kettle in the Schoepken. Kindling and wood needed to be cut so the laundry could be boiled the next day. Even the meal for the wash day was cooked the day before; usually it was pea soup or some other one-pot meal. Lots of preparations had to be made, since wash day came around about every three weeks. Wash day started early, about six AM. We did have a washing machine, which was operated manually. This was one of the occasions when tenant and owner worked and helped each other. As I got older it became my job to turn the wheel on the washing machine after school. My girlfriend would help, and we again would sing every song that entered into our minds.

In 1939, World War II started

On the first of September, 1939, World War II started, and my father, forty-one years of age with a family of six children to take care of, was one of the first ones to be drafted. He was soon wounded, shot through the knee, and could no longer serve as a solder. He was ordered to work in the "Schwelmer-Eisen-Werke" in the Ruhr Valley, the industrial region of Germany. This was about eighty miles from where we lived. He would come home every second weekend. This was always a special time for us. Our mother made us rake the garden paths and get enough clover for the chickens and dandelions for the rabbits to last over the weekend; we cleaned the pigsty and added fresh straw. About two in the afternoon we would take our pulling cart (Handwagen, Bollerwagen) and go to the train-station to welcome our dad. He and some other men from our town, who also were on duty in the Ruhr Valley, usually brought back big cartons full of shoes or other goods. People received rationing cards from the government not only for food, but also for shoes, etc. Since the stores in our town were practically empty, my father took these cards with him, name and shoe size written on them, and brought back several pairs of shoes, since they were more readily available in the big city.

Once home, the neighbors arrived to claim their goods. This was always a special time for me, because my father looked so important. Usually there were enough kids on hand to find takers for the shoes. When that commotion was dealt with and everyone had left, the big

Saturday wash-up could begin. The water in the big kettle was heated on the wood-burning stove, the zinc bathtub was brought into the kitchen, and one after the other we took our weekly bath. After each use, more hot water was added to the tub. Father would cut our toenails and fingernails if they needed it. The little ones, my sister Toni and I, would put on our nightgowns, which often were Sunday shirts the boys had outgrown. The others could still get dressed and go outside to play with their cousins next door and the other neighbor kids.

Supper meant leftovers from the midday meal, (our main meal) with maybe a pancake added or some milk soup. Each Sunday morning we walked to church. At the time, the farmers would still come in their horse-drawn coaches or buggies; older women wore their Sunday Tracht (traditional, regional dress) and the men always wore black. Some people would ride their bikes, and only the big landowners would drive a car, but most people walked. Everyone would attend church. On holidays the organ would roar and the congregation would sing with full voices as if to bring the house down. We children would take our place next to the main altar, kneeling on a carpet made of coconut fiber. It was hard on our knees, but we did not dare complain.

After church we went home while the men met in the "Wirtschaft" (neighborhood tavern) for a beer or a schnapps and talked. Mother was home and did the cooking. She had already been to early mass. Usually we started out with a beef noodle soup, a roast or sausage, (our piece of sausage was maybe two inches long), potatoes, gravy, and some vegetables. The best part of the meal was vanilla pudding with raspberry syrup. Every family in our area had pudding on Sunday. I know this; since there were no refrigerators, people cooled their pudding on the windowsill outside.

In the afternoon we had to go to catechism class. I believe now that my parents used this time for more than a nap. It gave them some assurance of privacy.

After walking home, we sometimes would get a piece of cake or some sweets and change from our Sunday clothes to our school clothes. Other times we would meet up with friends, play on the farms in the vicinity, or listened to someone play the accordion, (drums were improvised). Sometimes we went in the forest to pick flowers, mostly lupines and daisies. Other times we sat together and sang or played ball, etc. Soon it was time to milk the cows and time for us kids to go home. In the summertime we could play outside for a while after we had eaten a sandwich accompanied with a glass of buttermilk.

At times, after catechism, we would walk to my mother's homestead. Most of the farmers had Russian workers, who were prisoners of war or had been forced to come to Germany to work on the farms. Uncle Gerhard had inherited the farm, since he was the oldest in the family. Apparently he was not a good farmer, or so I learned later. In fact, he was a lousy farmer, but he was a good human being. He loved music and played the accordion well.

On Sundays, the Russian laborers came to Uncle Gerhard's farm to sing, play, and dance. We loved to watch them do their wild dances. There were also some Russian women among them. Wera, for instance, was a tall young woman. She helped my aunt, who was pregnant with her seventh child, with her chores. I remember seeing Wera standing in the huge kitchen by the tall windows, half covered with geraniums, looking out and crying. We all loved Wera, and she was treated as if she was part of the family. On her day off, Aunt Lisbeth, my mother's sister, who also helped on the farm during harvest-time, and Wera would come on their bikes and visit my mom. They had coffee, (made from grain), and a zwieback (crackers). They would talk and work on a dress for Wera or for one of us. All that was good, but it did not change the fact that Wera was taken off the field in Russia, not having a chance to even say good-bye to her family, and was taken to Germany to work.

Thinking about it in retrospect, I have concluded that the German people who lived at that time in history were as decent as any of the

Allies, who, in their self-righteousness and arrogance, condemned all the German people as war criminals. Be that as it may, the Germans who took advantage of their Russian laborers and mistreated them did get their reward when the war was over. The Russians killed them, using pitchforks.

At my father's homestead they had French prisoners of war to work for them. I remember one Sunday afternoon we were all sitting outside when the bombers appeared in the sky in great numbers. The roar became louder and louder. Uncle Bernd did not want to go inside, but the French prisoners insisted. They were very handsome, and my girl cousins, who were in their early twenties, were flirting with them; even a snotty kid like I could see that. These guys played the harmonica so beautifully.

In the wintertime we played "hide and go seek" on a farm in our area. We would hide among the animals in the barrens and stables. They kept the place comfortably warm. Other times we played games in the enormously large kitchen, which had a potbelly stove in the center. There was room for everyone.

One day, word came that my Uncle Anton had been killed in Sicily. One of my aunts was married to a Dutchman and lived in Holland. Somehow, she had been notified. Now everyone was waiting for her to come to attend the service. We hoped the farmers on both sides of the border would try to help her get across. It was evening. We were praying the rosary when someone knocked on the window. It was my aunt. She had successfully made the crossing to attend the services for her fallen brother.

The Ruhr Valley, because of its industry, became a target for bombing. Women and children were evacuated to the countryside. They lived in makeshift quarters or with other families, hoping to escape the bombings. All the houses were kept dark; the windows were cowered so no light could escape, and there were no streetlights. We would hold hands, tell scary stories, and pretend not to hear the airplanes above. Of course, we were not frightened; we just ran home as fast as we could. When the alarm sounded during the night, we rushed into the basement, carrying our pillow and blanket with us, and continued to sleep on bundles of straw. Sometimes we went outside and watched how the Ruhr-Valley was burning. The sky in the distance was aglow. We worried, because our father worked there. The roar of the bombers sounded like one hundred gas-powered lawnmowers working at the same time.

When the alarm sounded while we were in school, we would all be herded into the ditches around the schoolyard. They were about two meters deep and two meters wide, dug out for our protection. We could see the airplanes above, and at times they would fly so low that we could see the pilot in the cockpit.

One day, my sister and I went to the maker of wooden shoes to try on a new pair of wooden shoes. A little more wood needed to be chiseled out at the toes to make them fit. In our area almost everyone wore wooden shoes. His daughter gave us an apple as we chatted. We happily went on our way. The next morning, the airplanes flew especially low. In the afternoon we heard the bad news. The young girl who had given us the apple had been shot and killed while milking the cow; the cow was killed also.

Another time, I was getting my Saturday bath when everyone ran outside to see this big plane going in circles and coming closer. I got out of the tub in a hurry, put some clothes on and also ran outside. The plane finally landed in a field. Big pieces of metal had fallen off. The doctor was already there. The pilot was placed on the metal, and we were chased away. I do not know what happened to him. A few days later, another solder had been discovered in a hayloft. I saw him walking between two farmers passing by our house. They said he was a Canadian. He was brought to the mayor's office.

I do not remember the Crystal Night, since I was too young. I remember one brutality. It was on my first communion day. We were playing outside when a couple of solders kicked an old man to the ground, dragged him over the gravel, and pushed him into the train. I don't know why, but I did not tell my parents about it. I still see the picture in front of me.

My mother took chances, more than most people did. The Jewish people who were still in town would come to us for vegetables. My mother would go into the garden, cut spinach and other vegetables, wrap them in newspaper, and hand them to them. The Jewish lady would always have a few candies for us. They could have been jelly beans; at least they looked like jelly beans. At twilight, we were sent outside to see if anyone was on the street. When the streets were clear, the Jewish lady walked behind the tall hedge in back of our garden into the rye field and walked home.

The war begins to have an impact on our lives

Due to the war, we had less school. The time was occupied picking potato bugs off the potato plants. Whole fields had been infested. It was believed the Allies dropped them by the planeloads. We had not had potato bugs before.

One Saturday, we went again to the train station. Father did not come. The other men carried his few belongings. They asked if mom was home. They walked with us to the house and informed our mom that dad had been picked up because, they said, "He could not keep his mouth shut and demanded better treatment for the Russian prisoners. So, they picked him up." No one knew where he was. After about six weeks he came back. He had been digging one-man holes near Aachen. Among his few belongings was part of a Puppenstube (dollhouse) he had been working on for us for Christmas.

The Sunday after Easter was Weisser Sonntag (Wit Sunday). Traditionally, children had their first communion on this day. In 1944, it was my special day. We had had our religious instructions in school and also after school at the convent. Catholic and Lutheran schools ware separate, but they were all public schools. My place at the table was especially decorated, with pansies all around the place setting. There was a candle in the center. My dress was my sister's communion dress. It was navy blue and had a fancy collar around the neck. I did get a new flower wreath of tiny, white, artificial roses to wear on my head. I was happy. We walked to the ancient church, where I lined up with my other classmates. There was a mass and the sermon was especially tailored for us children. We took our first communion, said our prayers, and sang while the organ was playing and the big bells were ringing. After mass we all walked home, parents, godparents, sisters, and brothers, all anticipating a nice meal, which the neighbors had prepared.

It was one of the duties the neighbors had, helping each other on special occasions, and first communion certainly was such an occasion. In the afternoon we played with the other kids in the neighborhood and also showed off the gifts we had received. My godfather gave me a crucifix which, sixty-five years later still hangs over the door in my kitchen. Ours was the last class that had their first communion in the old church. We were born in 1936.

On the 20th of March, 1945, several bombs fell on our town. A few people were killed. It was like a prelude of what was ahead. The next day, the twenty-first of March, and the first day of spring, we were playing Easter bunny, making eggs out of wet sand, when we heard the bombers approach. They came in great numbers, making an awful noise. We ran to the makeshift bunker behind the garden, made of huge sewer pipes covered with dirt. There were kids and grownups, sitting side by side on wooden boards. We could hear the bombs fall, coming closer. Everyone was praying aloud, "Our father who art in heaven." Someone shouted, "Hold your ears tight and open your mouth" The ground was shaking. Kids were crying; people screaming, and the noise was terrible. Finally it calmed down. Slowly, everyone crawled out of the bunker. Our house was standing and so was the neighbor's, but the city was burning, and the church towers were gone. Houses across the field, where my schoolmates lived, were flattened.

My oldest brother, who was seventeen years old at the time, had been drafted to the Eastern Front. He and a few other young boys had fled, realizing that the war was lost. They saw the refugees fleeing ahead of the Russians, pulling their few belongings behind them. All the cities were bombed and burning; death everywhere. I remember my mother pleading with my brother to go back to the front because, she said, "The Nazis will hang you if they catch you." The boys did not go back, but two lost their lives under the bombs.

My brother, and everyone who felt they could help, went to town to dig out the living and the dead, while the planes were still flying low and still shooting at them. Word came of who had been killed, and of who was still making noise in the basement but could not be reached. In the evening my mother went with a lady friend to look for her son, who was an apprentice in a cobbler's shop. She came back, visibly shaken, and said that they had found Bernie among the many others who had been killed and brought to the Turner Hall (athletic club). She said they found him, still wearing his leather apron, while the rats were nibbling on his ear.

The next morning, my uncle Gerhard came with his horse and wagon. He had come the long way around town to evacuate us. We picked a few belongings at random. My younger sister, still in bed, was picked up with her feather bed and put on the wagon. Later we looked for her, not realizing that she already was on the wagon. The wagon was set in motion. We saw a flatbed with bodies. The mother of one of my schoolmates was sitting on a chair among the dead. Her daughter, my schoolmate, had her foot sticking out from under the blanket. All were dead and were taken to the cemetery, which had also been bombed. The airplanes were still flying low, dropping bombs or shooting at the civilians. At my uncle's farm there were many people, all kinds of people. The German army was still present; there were old men who had been drafted and who tried to hide, hoping it would all be over soon. We all slept on straw in the big stable attached to the house. No one ever changed clothes. The bathroom was somewhere out there in the bushes. At night we could hear the tanks rolling. The grownups were wondering if they were German or the enemy tanks. The able-bodied men were in town digging out the people from under the rubble, burying the dead in mass graves, or helping the wounded. When my brother came home one evening he said they had found my teacher dead.

After a few days the German army was gone, and the English tanks rolled in. My mother had a white pillowcase attached at the top of a beanpole. She walked toward the tanks, followed by a bunch of raggedy-looking kids and old men and women. The soldiers were English. They made us line up, machine guns pointing at us; some of the solders checked out the house and the surroundings. Finally they brought out some ham, looked for eggs in the chicken coop, and asked the women to make them something to eat. That was a relief. It appeared they were not going to harm us. I don't remember how we all were fed. Luckily, it was a warm spring, and we could sleep under the open sky.

The next morning, I remember I heard kids laughing. I went toward the barn and noticed an English solder giving my sister a push on the swing. These guys had made a swing for us using a heavy rope that they had tied around the rafters in the barn; they added a board at the bottom of the loop, and the swing was ready for action. Another solder came with a can of candies.

The bombing had stopped for good, and we planned on going back home to our place, hoping it would still be there. My brother loaded the wagon and soon we took off. The horses seemed to know the way. My wooden shoes were worn thin, and as we moved through town where the rubble had been cleared the stones would poke through my soles; mud seeped in and caked my socks. I had a tough time keeping up. Devastation was all around us.

When we made it home, the house was still there; windows and doors had been shot through, but we had shelter. The fields and meadows had deep grooves created by the tanks crisscrossing them. The English solders had made our "Schoepkin" into a field kitchen. There was food, and we could smell it. A bunch of kids watched them cutting bread. A couple of slices fell in the mud. We all jumped to fetch the bread, but a soldier, with his heavy boot, stumped it into the mud, almost stepping on our hands, laughing.

A few days later, my father came. He had hitchhiked and walked from the Ruhr Valley all the way home. There was no transportation. All the railroad tracks were bombed. He was a sad sight and looked like a skeleton. He had contracted kidney disease and was 100 percent disabled. We realized our father was seriously ill. I would crawl into bed with him to keep him company and to keep each other warm. He would say, "Let's sing." We would always sing the same song, "Schone, o Herr, schone dein Volk" (protect us, Lord, protect thy people). My brother Hermann would climb the trees in the forest and get the pigeons before they could fly out of the nest. My mother made soup for my father. He needed something nourishing.

Things began to normalize, or so we thought. The war had ended. My sister Lissi went to work on a farm; my oldest brother, Jup, started his apprenticeship as an auto mechanic; my oldest sister, Gertrud, went to live with the nuns to learn cooking. That left three of us kids at home. Slowly the house was being repaired. My cousin Hein, next door, finally came home from the prisoner of war camp. I only remember that he hallucinated a lot and was fed oatmeal cooked in water.

Once a week I would go to the farm where my sister worked to fetch a quart of milk. One day my sister said, "Come early and sit through dinner; maybe there will be some leftovers, and you might get it." Big platters of pancakes and bacon were placed on the table along with pitchers of buttermilk. I sat in the corner while everyone was eating up a storm. I saw the stacks of pancakes get shorter. Finally the farm lady said, "That is enough now; save some for Waldman" (the dachshund). My heart sank. There were no pancakes left for me. My sister looked at me in disappointment.

In the meantime, all the refugees from the eastern sectors started to arrive. These people had survived the war, but after the war, millions were kicked out of their homeland. I learned later that the Allies had agreed at Potsdam and Yalta at the Black Sea conference to give this German land to the Russians, Poles, and Czechs. The German people had lived in these regions for hundreds of years. These people had been given notice at 9:00 AM to get out by 2:00 PM. Everyone was forced to move west in wagons, on foot, pulling carts, etc. By now it was winter. The ice on the lakes and rivers was not yet thick enough to hold the weight of these endless tracks, and many, trying to get to safety, drowned in the icy waters.

All were driven into the devastated heart of Europe, called Germany. The local people were not too keen to take them in. They already were over crowded with all the people from the bombed-out cities. They came by the thousands, foraging food wherever they could find it. In the spring, neighbors took turns keeping watch in the fields with wooden clubs to protect the crops just planted. People were begging for one potato or a piece of pig skin, etc. They exchanged jewelry, linens, crystal, even wedding rings for a couple of eggs. We would walk to grandmother's house, and she would give us a spoonful of lard to take home. My uncle, who had inherited the farm, had a big family himself, and the farm help had families too who expected to get paid with food to take home. I was a very skinny kid and would go from farm to farm to beg for an egg or whatever they could give me. When I had received something, I would go to my sister, who was in the ditch waiting for me. I would give her whatever I had been given and go on to the next farmer. Even though we knew the farmers and they knew who we were, we were often sent away because we had no goods to exchange.

I had lice. Most people had lice, especially children, but they sure liked me. They seemed to crawl out of my skull. My sister and I had our hair cut off. Our heads were rubbed with turpentine. It would burn like hell, and it killed the lice, but it did not kill the eggs, so the procedure had to be repeated every two weeks or so. We had little schooling. The buildings that were still somewhat intact were occupied by the English soldiers. During the day we would go unto the fields that had already been harvested to dig the soil, hoping to find just one more potato. We were not alone. Whole groups of people skimmed the land for all kinds of edibles. The forests swarmed with people picking berries, while the Allied soldiers cut down the big oak trees and hauled them away.

Finally, my father found a solution to our bartering problem. We started to make schnapps. The farmers brought us the grain (coarsely ground rye), and we added water and yeast covered the big tubs with blankets to force fermentation. We made alcohol by the buckets. The alcohol would drip from a tube, cooled in a barrel of cold water, into the gas mask that had been given to every family for protection. They now served as filters, and the schnapps would drip through the gas mask into a glass jar. The schnapps would be filled into big milk cans, which we kids transported on the pulling cart (Bollerwagen) to the dairy. There, we would meet the milkman, who exchanged cans with us. The cans we brought home contained bread, flour, eggs, salted pork, ham, you name it. One time us kids sneaked into the Schoepkin and sucked on the gas mask filters. Of course the alcohol made us drunk and sick. We did that only once; we had learned our lesson. The main thing was, we had food on the table, and we had food and schnapps to exchange for soap, combs, matches, coal, wood, yarn, and whatever else we needed. Matches were very valuable. The neighbors took turns to keep one fire going. In the morning everyone came with their buckets with some kindling in it to get the fire, rush home and start the fire in the stove. This arrangement worked, and people took it in stride.

In the "Bollerwagen" we transported everything from coal, grain, potatoes, apples, small pigs, and rabbits in the spring. The Bollerwagen served also as a toy. When the automobile took over, the "Bollerwagen" was dismantled. We divided the four axles among us four sisters; they now serve as candleholders, and I was happy to get one.

My brothers were very good poachers. They would trap rabbits and even brought home deer. This was very dangerous and illegal but it helped us survive. I believe the forester closed an eye every now and then for us.

I remember one Sunday morning in church (the Turner Hall, or athletic club, which now serving as a church), my brother never kneeled during the service. He stood there like a pole. At home I found out why. He had caught a rabbit on the way to church, had attached it to his suspensors and had it hung inside his trouser leg. That explained why he could not kneel.

I remember another incident. My girlfriend and I were looking in the garbage pile for whatever could be of value to us. We found a knitted sweater. It was torn and was full of human waste. We fought over it. She won, washed it, unraveled it, and knitted herself a nice, warm sweater. All the knots on the inside made it a very thick sweater. I remember I was very, very jealous.

That was not the only time I was jealous. My girlfriend had relatives in Duesseldorf. Because, they believed that the countryside was safer than the city, they had spent much time with my girlfriend's family. Every time they came they brought another doll or clothes for the doll or some kind of toy. I had no doll. My brother had fashioned a birch log for me, and that was my doll. One day my girlfriend was taking her dolls for an outing in her doll carriage. I asked if I could push the carriage. She said no. I was angry and thought of ways to get even. I mentioned that the dolls could get plenty of fresh air standing under the tree. She agreed and placed her carriage under the tree, next to a bench. I climbed on the bench, grabbed a branch of the tree, swung back and forth, and then "accidentally" kicked the carriage with the full force of my legs. The buggy fell over, the dolls rolled out, and the pillows got all soiled. I apologized, knowing full well I wanted this to happen, and derived great pleasure from having succeeded.

Another event that stands out in my mind is the day the church bells were returned. During the war the bells had all been taken out of the steeple to be melted down for cannons. Luckily for our bells, the war was over before the bells were melted down in the smelter. I do not remember when the bells were hauled away; but I sure remember when they returned. Everyone who could walk joined the procession toward the church yard. The bells were lined up according to size, decorated with pine garlands. A new church had been built on the spot where the old church once stood. All the huge old Linden trees were gone also. The brass band played, and people were singing "Holy God, We Praise Thy Name." The bells were the communicators of their time. They rang for every special event. They also rang when the last prisoner of war came home from Russia. Again, everyone who could make it went to the train station to welcome him. I remember people laughing and crying. This was in 1951, six years after the war ended.

In spite of it all, I did not think of these times as bad times. We had few toys, but we were very inventive. For instance, in the winter we played "store." We would break the ice in the ditches and pretend it was crystal. We looked at a piece from all sides and sold the different "figurines" as horses, dolls, flowers, or whatever we imagined them to be. For compensation we shook hands. When it was time to go to bed, we would take our brick out of the baking tube of the wood-burning stove and wrap it in a towel; it became our bed warmer.

1948: The situation begins to improve

Finally, in 1948, things began to look up. The old Reichsmark was changed to the new Deutschmark. We had no more lice, and there was food on the table. School attendance was regular. We were with sixty-five kids in one classroom. Even the windowsills were used as desks. Some of the classmates were refugees from eastern Germany, the provinces which were taken away from Germany and now belonged to Russia, Poland, or Czechoslovakia. The wide ditches around the schoolyard were filled. Young people attended dances. We made no more schnapps. My father had recovered and had a job. My second brother, Hermann, was half way through his apprenticeship learning the butcher and sausage-making trade. On Saturdays, he would bring a roast or some other meat products home. We no longer stood in endless lines for a loaf of bread, just to be told they ran out before it was our turn. We again had two pigs in the Schoepken and coal and potatoes in the basement for the winter. Life was good.

I graduated from school in 1950 and worked in different places

I graduated from public school in 1950. My father took me out of school a half year early because my mother had eczema on her hands and needed help at home. I heard him say many times that it was important for the boys to learn at least a trade, but the girls would get married and did not need an education. I never gave it a second thought and did not object.

When my mother's hands improved, I worked on a farm for a few months. I liked that, learned much, and was with Mother Nature when doing my work.

Sooner or later I needed another job. Our neighbor lady had a sister who was a nun in a big hospital in Gelsenkirchen-Horst. My cousin, who was also my girlfriend, and I applied for a job, and we were hired. She worked at the reception desk, and I worked in the kitchen. Leaving home for the first time and going to a strange place was not easy. We had to take the train and keep track of every stop on the way to make sure we would get off at the right place.

We were taken to our room, which was a large room in the attic. We shared the room with three other girls. Each one of us had one large drawer for our belongings and maybe room for three coat hangers in the closet. The bathroom was in the hallway.

It all was so new. I believe I rode the elevator for the first time in that hospital. The girls were nice. I learned how to cook and even had to butcher chickens. Everything was done right there on the premises. The nuns had a huge garden and their own bakery and laundry. One could often hear them sing in the chapel on Sunday afternoons. I loved to go and listen to the nuns sing the vesper. To this day I like that kind of chanting music.

After a couple of months, my cousin received word that she could start working in the textile factory in our hometown. Of course, the pay was much better. So she left, and I stayed behind. I stayed a year, but I always had the urge to go farther away from home to see if I could actually handle myself and survive.

I went home for a short while and applied for a job in Krefeld, located on the Lower Rhine River. As a child, I had often dreamed about working on the shores of the Rhine, selling vegetables, the Rhine in the background being one thousand meters wide.

Wow! That was a mighty river.

Well, I did see the Rhine in Krefeld. I worked there for a nose, throat, and ear specialist. I was the second maid. The first maid also came from my hometown. We had a tiny room, again in the attic. This family had two children. The girl was very spoiled and told me, "Clean my shoes. What are you here for?" I did not like that, but I had very little self-esteem and just took it. The doctor was very nice and tried to encourage me to learn and do better. He would correct my German, since I had spoken mostly Low German at home. I appreciated the help. His wife was the lady of the house, and she enjoyed letting me know it.

Again, I stayed a year and went home.

My parents had a job lined up for me, and I was to go and introduce myself. Instead of going there, I went to a newspaper stand and inquired about placing on ad. The lady was very helpful, and before I knew it, I had placed a job-seeking ad in a Stuttgart newspaper. I had read and heard about mountains but had never seen any. I figured Stuttgart is far south, and they must have mountains there.

When I came home and informed my parents of my plans, they could not believe it. My behavior was unacceptable and embarrassing to my parents. After all, they had negotiated a job for me with these people in town.

My father said he would not give the money for the train ride, and, therefore, I was stuck in my hometown. I informed him that I had already inquired and could fetch a ride with some truck drivers, of whom one was the brother of a schoolmate.

Everything was arranged. All my father could do was talk to these guys to take good care of me and see to it that I got to the right place. Both young men came from reputable families.

So, I went; the first one in our family to go that far away. I did not dare cry but was scared stiff. I had never seen an Autobahn, bridges with trains going under and over them, and hills. To think … one could stand on solid ground and be higher than the chimney of a house.

Oh my, was I green. In Karlsruhe, I had to fetch a train to Stuttgart. The biggest surprise came when I heard the people speak, and I could not understand them. How could that language be German? I found the Metzgerei (the butcher shop) that was supposed to be my place of employment. It was located in a beautiful area, hills all around. I liked it but had to learn much. Everything was different—the language, the food, working conditions, everything.

They had two children, a boy and a girl. The little boy was very cute, and I enjoyed him very much. In fact, his name was Rolf, and when our son was born ten years later, and we were searching for a name, I asked my husband if we could name him Rolf, because that little rascal had taught me to love and appreciate children. Rolf became Ralph, but that was OK.

This was a big household consisting of the couple as heads of household, two children, a grandfather, a journeyman, and an apprentice. Often there were relatives helping out. I was expected to cook for all of them, clean their quarters, do the laundry, etc. The Schwabian people have a reputation as hard workers, and I have to say that is true. I learned much. Everyone was very good to me. The pay was minimal, but I could eat all the meat and sausage I wanted. Sunday was my day off, and I would meet with a couple of girls I had met who worked in the bakery.

I went home once. My brother, Jup, who had switched from being an auto mechanic to a tool and die maker, worked in the textile factory. He informed me that soon there would be jobs available. He would notify me by telegram. If I wanted to work in the factory to make more money, I would have to come home at once or the jobs would be taken by others.

At that time, residents in Vreden commuted to Holland and the Ruhr Valley to work. Jobs in our area were very, very scarce.

I went back to Stuttgart. A couple of months later the telegram arrived. "Come at once," it read. I informed the lady of the house. She was visibly upset and informed me that I had to live by the rules and had to give at least one month's notice. What was I supposed to do?

I sat down in my room that same evening and wrote a letter to the CEO of the textile company. I did not know his name or the address of the factory, but I hoped the letter would reach him just the same. I explained my situation and asked for understanding. I would try my best not to disappoint him should he hire me. I closed by saying, "Should the letter end up in the paper basket, I would not consider the time it took to write it wasted, for it had given me a chance to practice and improve my German."

The letter went in the mail, and a couple of weeks later I received a reply confirming that a job was waiting for me. I was happy; now I could start working and saving for the Atlantic crossing to try my luck in America.

Working in the factory was again a new experience. The stench of oil and grease of these textile machines was so strong that it made me gag. Every day I felt nauseated, and I really struggled with that. The hair was always full of cotton dust. It often was very hot in these halls. It was not very pleasant, to say the least. I also had trouble working piecework.

I could not keep up with the rest of the girls. However, I did earn more money than working in the household. I gave some of it to my parents and saved the rest.

My brother, Hermann, had left for America in November of 1954. We took him to the train station. He said, "You take me to the train, and I will pick you up in America."

Leaving home to come to America

My father had lived in America from 1923 until 1925. He often told us about his experiences and impressions of the New World. I believe now that his view of the United States was too rosy, but at the time he had just lived through the Second World War and had returned to a bombed-out city as a 100 percent disabled man. We listened to his stories, and my brother, at the age of twenty-one, left for America. Two years later, on May 5, 1956, at the age of twenty I traveled with my girlfriend to Cuxhaven. I walked on the ship called *Italia*, and she stayed behind.

I am getting ahead of myself. I was always eager to see the world and had lived in Gelsenkirchen, Krefeld, and Stuttgart, doing housework. Earning very little money, I soon realized I would never earn enough to pay for the ocean voyage to America. I began working in a factory and saved my money.

Soon, my visa arrived. I barely could pay for the fare. My parents wanted to help me pay, but I insisted on paying my own way. I paid a carpenter twenty Deutsch Marks to make a wooden box for me, which would have to do instead of a suitcase. Time of departure was getting closer, and my anxiety was growing. It was time to say good-bye.

Saying good-bye to my working companions was not too hard. One of them let it be known that I was pretty stupid for wasting 850 Deutsch Marks on a trip across the ocean, when I could have used the money to buy myself an electric sewing machine.

Some of the neighbors came to the house to say good-bye; to the others, I went. One neighbor had made potato pancakes, one of my favorite dishes. I had trouble getting them down; they just stuck in my throat.

My two older sisters had become mothers a couple of months ago, and their babies were so cute. My oldest brother, who had always been my big brother while my father was doing his duty in the war, tried to help me with everything like he had always done. I don't remember too much about my younger sister at the time. My father kept on saying, "I wish I could give you my knowledge of the English language." My mother, on the other hand, was just quiet.

The time came to put my few belongings into the wooden box. To my surprise, there was much space left to fill. I took some old "Christliche Familie," which was a weekly newspaper I enjoyed reading, and placed them at the bottom of the box. On top of the newspapers I packed my few belongings, among them a crucifix, which I had received from my godfather at my first communion, and a picture of the Virgin Mary. All was safe in the box. My large leather purse held my tickets and a little extra money tucked away. My clothes for the next morning were hanging on the closet door. All was ready, and I went to bed, trying to keep from sobbing.

The next day, this was it. I shook hands with my father, sister, brother, and my mom, (hugging and kissing openly was not done in northern Germany). All of us cried inside but tried to hide it. My girlfriend had arrived, and the two of us took off. About a block down the street I turned around and saw my mother clinging to the garden post. I believe it was the most intense pain I ever experienced.

We boarded the bus filled with students and commuters. I hoped they would not look at me, for my face was a sad mess. We transferred onto the train that took us to Cuxhaven. There were all kinds of people, some crying. I said good-bye to my girlfriend and walked onto the ship.

I found my cabin and learned the upper berth was mine. My wooden box was already there.

I walked back on deck. My girlfriend was nowhere to be seen. The ship pulled away from the pier. All of us stood at the railing, looking back until land was out of sight. It was May 6, 1956.

By now, it was almost dinnertime. I had not lost my appetite. Pork roast and gravy, red cabbage, and potatoes were being served. I also was introduced to something I believed to be grapes. They turned out to be black olives. What a surprise!

People at the table were friendly. I actually enjoyed myself until I became violently ill. I believed I was seasick, but the steward insisted on calling the doctor. Dr.Wesselhoeft examined me and informed me that I had an acute appendicitis infection and that I needed to be operated on at once. Within an hour or so I climbed upon the operating table. When I woke up, I found myself in the ship's hospital. A young nurse was sitting at my bedside. All this happened before we had reached Le Havre and Southampton.

Actually, I felt pretty good. I had never been fussed over so much before. After a couple of days I was transferred to a first-class cabin, where I had my own poster bed. The captain came to visit, and so did other passengers on board. The nurse would at times sit down to talk to me. My, did I fit the description of a greenhorn. I could not speak a word of English but was not worried. Ignorance was bliss.

The sea was rough, and the sandbag on my wound would move every time the ship rolled from side to side or back and forth.

After eleven days at sea, we reached New York. People were excited, walking on deck, looking at the Statue of Liberty. I too could walk again. The doctor had notified my brother in Milwaukee, who in turn had phoned people in New York, who had agreed to get me off the ship.

While I was waiting for them, something funny happened, or so it seems in retrospect. Someone came up to me and informed me that I would be on "television." Television sounded so much like "Teller wischen," which means "washing dishes" in German. I began to wonder how these people could tell, looking at me, that I had worked as a maid. Was it that obvious? I began to protest and let them know I was not interested in "television."

I do not know until this day, whether or not I was shown on television. It does not matter. The lady, designated to get me off the ship had arrived. This was May 16, 1956. She was so friendly and helpful. We went through customs. The officer lifted the lid of my wooden box and looked at the crucifix and the picture of the Virgin Mary; then he motioned to close the lid, and off the ship we went. The lady had my box shipped to my brother to Milwaukee. The two of us rode the streetcar through the big city of New York to the big apartment house that she and her husband managed. There were many black people on the streetcar. In Germany I had only seen a few.

While entering the huge apartment complex, a little girl in the elevator said, "Hi." The lady said to me, "Say, 'hi'." I complied, not knowing what it meant.

That evening I was introduced to steak, and a big one at that. There was more meat on my plate than we had had at home with the whole family. The man of the house turned the television on, and we watched wrestling.

The next morning the lady took me to the airport. I carried a newspaper clipping about the arrival of the *Italia*. I was mentioned as "having been able to walk off the ship under my own power."

The stewardess kept on eye on me, for every time the propeller plane landed and I got out of my seat, she pushed me back gently and said, "Sit." Finally, we landed in Milwaukee, and my brother was there to welcome me.

All this happened more than fifty years ago. This is just one story of seven million people who left Germany to come to the USA.

Starting life in Milwaukee in 1956

Ten days had passed since my appendix had been removed. I was in pretty good condition but not well enough to start a household for my brother and myself. My brother had brought me to my father's cousin, who had a farm in Burlington, Wisconsin. Uncle Bernd, as we called him, and his wife, Helen, spoke German very well. They had some cattle, chickens, a big vegetable garden, etc. The windmill, so typical on American farms, furnished the water for family and beasts alike. These cousins were very good to me. Still, farm life in America was very different from the way I had experienced it back home in Germany, and I had to adjust.

Sunday morning we went to St. Mary's Church. To my surprise, the stained-glass windows had been donated by German immigrants, and the dedication was written in German. I was introduced to several people, all of them cousins a couple of generations removed. In the afternoon we visited another of my father's cousins, who lived at the homestead in Lyons, Wisconsin My father's uncle had immigrated in the 1880s. His name was carved into the stone steps of the main entrance of his Victorian farmhouse. It was strange to see my last name right there, somewhat eternalized, thousands of miles away from home. I was very much impressed by Uncle Toni's young daughters, who were riding the horses bareback.

After about a week, my brother came to fetch me. He had rented an apartment near the shoreline of Michigan Lake, but the neighborhood was somewhat run-down. He was careful with the money, and this was all he could afford at the time. The furniture was supposed to be delivered the next day. We stayed at his friend's house overnight.

The next day, my brother dropped me off at the apartment house. All I had was a bucket, which served as a stool, to sit on and wait for the furniture. I looked around me and saw the dirty walls and wondered how I could clean them instead of just sitting on the bucket, waiting. I dared to step out into the hallway. A friendly lady approached me. I motioned to her, using my arms and legs and everything else, to make her understand that I wanted to wash the walls. She understood and came back with a small stepladder, some old rags, and detergent. I let her know through sign language that I was grateful. I started to wash the walls. When my brother arrived from work he could not believe that I had communicated to the landlady what I wanted and had almost completed washing the walls of one room. The furniture arrived a little later. This was our beginning. I had a bed; my brother slept on a bed couch. We had a table, a couple of chairs, and a few dishes and pots from the Salvation Army.

We settled in, and then it was time to look for a job. My brother had befriended an elderly couple. The man was German; she was American. The man went to the Knickerbocker Hotel with me. The housekeeper there was German. She hired me as a chambermaid. I was the only white girl among black ladies. I found this all very interesting. These ladies were very good to me and helped me learn the American way of doing things. I tried to learn English by asking "name?" and pointing to an object, and they would tell me, table, chair, window, floor, etc. I wrote these words down the way they sounded and tried to memorize them. I often mixed them up and called the chair the ceiling, or vice versa.

After some time, a family living on the upper floor of the hotel in a very luxurious apartment, overlooking Lake Michigan, asked if I could help them by serving food at a cocktail party. The lady was Jewish and spoke German fluently. They provided a cocktail dress for me, and that very evening I passed platters with all kinds of goodies around. Most of the items I did not recognize. There were many people present and not enough chairs for them to sit on. I had never been to a party where people held a drink in one hand and balanced a plate with food in the other. They looked quite happy, and I had the impression that most of them were very well off.

The lady of the house had sent a request to the housekeeping department asking for me to help her clean the cupboards. I arrived, and she said, "Here is a fresh glass of orange juice. It is going to be hot today, and it will do you good." I have to admit, no lady had ever done that for me in Germany.

We started to take the dishes out of the cupboards when she said, "Be careful, this is Meissen porcelain." It did not mean anything to me. I had never heard of it before. She was surprised and told me that I, as a German, should know what Meissen is. She said that once you learn to speak English well, you will sound no different than a professor who happened to come from Germany. We would most likely both still have an accent. The only difference would be that he knew more, but I could also learn much, if I wanted to. That talk left a big impression on me.

She made me understand that I was as good as the next person and that it was up to me to set goals and try to reach them. So far, people had often talked down to me, and I had very little self-esteem. I slowly began to understand what she had tried to convey. This was America, and everyone could be what he or she wanted to be. To this day I am grateful to this lady and will be as long as I live.

I had worked at the Knickerbocker Hotel for several months when I landed a job at the Downing cardboard box factory. I was placed in a department where there were men only. I had to take the folded boxes off the conveyer belt and stack them unto a pallet. I was paid male wages but learned soon that they had read my name as Mario instead of Maria. I paid that extra money back over a short period of time. Equal rights did not yet exist.

I met some German girls at work, and we became friends. We still write or call each other at least four times a year. All did well, and the children went on to college. We have also visited each other—all this fifty-some years later.

My brother had a good-paying job, and I also made good money. We looked for another apartment in a better neighborhood. The owners of these flats came from Yugoslavia. They lived downstairs, and we lived upstairs. We bought a few more pieces of furniture. On holidays, we had open house at our home. Any German immigrant who had no place to go was invited. I learned how to cook a turkey with all the trimmings. Our American parents, this was the name we had given to the couple who had helped me get the job at the hotel, lived close to the University of Wisconsin. They rented out an apartment to a professor and his wife from Switzerland, and rooms to a couple of brothers from Germany, who had been prisoners of war in Russia, and an American naval officer. In the evening, they would gather in the living room. We had the most interesting discussions. I, being only twenty-one years old, sat among them and listened. I learned much, but mostly I learned not to be afraid to speak my mind.

All these people spent Thanksgiving and Christmas Eve with us, including a couple of friends of my brother, and my girlfriends. We had good times. In the summertime my brother would take me along to Moose Lake, also known as Karl Schurz Park. Wisconsin has many lakes, one more beautiful than the other, surrounded by a hilly countryside. Moose Lake was where the Germans would meet. We could buy good food there for a reasonable price. Often music played for our dancing pleasure. I learned how to swim in Moose Lake and was no longer afraid to be pushed off the raft floating offshore. Most of the visitors were immigrants like us. They had come from all regions of Europe. All had nothing and therefore nothing to lose. They all tried hard to get ahead somehow. We had much fun. Often we would meet at the Old Heidelberg, dance late into the night, then stop for breakfast, pizza, or a cheeseburger before we went home.

Yet, I wanted to see more of America. My girlfriend and I went on a tour to Colorado. We saw the majestic Rocky Mountains, rode a horse on a ranch; visited a ghost town and crossed the Royal Gorge on a tall hanging bridge, among other things. God, the world is beautiful, we concluded.

I was hit by the travel bug.

My journey to Hawaii and my early beginnings there

My brother gave me a suitcase for Christmas, and on March 21, 1960, he took me to the airport in Milwaukee, and off to Hawaii I went. Again, I was scared, but not scared enough to stop me from going.

The plane was a propeller machine that took me to San Francisco. I arrived late at night, went to the information desk at the airport and asked how to go about getting a reasonable hotel. The man called a cab, and the driver took me to the Palace Hotel on Market Street, one of the most luxurious hotels in the city. I wondered about the expense. The next morning I had breakfast in the Garden Room. I ordered oatmeal, because it was the cheapest item on the menu. I walked out of the hotel onto Market Street and took a bus, not knowing where it would take me. I ended up at the Cliff House on Ocean Beach, a wide beach with big waves. It was a sight to behold. I walked for a while then got on the bus again. This time we went through Golden Gate Park. I debarked at the Japanese Teagarden. This again was something totally new, different, and beautiful. I ordered a tea, and I believe I did get a fortune cookie.

Somehow I made it to Fisherman's Warf. Standing at a corner waiting for the light to change, an old pickup truck stopped. The window at the driver's seat was rolled down. A young girl, wearing a tank top, her long hair flowing, looked out and yelled at the top of her voice, "I feel so good inside!" I thought this was really fantastic and decided San Francisco was a great city.

In the evening, I joined a nightclub tour of North Beach. Among the stops was Finokious, a well-known nightclub. Back on the bus, a man explained to me that all those well-dressed, beautiful women in the show had been men. I could not believe it. Why would those men dress up like women? My, was I green.

The next morning, I went to the airport and continued my journey to Hawaii. Next to me on the plane sat a man of Italian descent who owned a restaurant at the pier in Santa Cruz as well as a fish processing plant. He was on his way to Manila, Tokyo, Hong Kong, and other exotic places to buy fish. We talked, and he asked what I planned to do in Hawaii. I said work but had no specific training in any field. He said, "Stand up." He looked me over and decided I should be a stewardess. He wanted to help me because he said he could not see his daughters going off to Hawaii to work, being that it is so far away from home. It would worry him. He shook his head, mumbling, "She comes half way around the world."

We landed at the Honolulu International Airport, which was nothing more than a landing strip with a few metal sheds to handle customers, and some huts here and there where the natives sold flower leis.

The Italian man from the plane gave me the dates, addresses, and telephone numbers of the places he would visit. He said if I needed money or anything else not to hesitate to contact him. He would help me out. Then he rented a room for me at the Waikikian Hotel and ordered a taxi. I was on my way while he had to wait to get the connection to continue his travels.

I was impressed with the Polynesian-style hotel—its tropical plants, flowers, and exotic birds sitting in the trees. The women walked around, with flowers in their hair, in long, colorful dresses. I later learned they were called muumuus. I walked to the beach; palms swaying in the wind. This was Hawaii as I had seen it in my dreams.

In my excitement, I kept on walking along Kalakaua Avenue, instead of going back to the hotel. Before I realized it, I was lost. "Where was my hotel," I wondered, "and what was it called?" I asked an elderly man, who said he lived across the street from the hotel where all the stewardesses were staying, and he said, "It is probably the hotel where you are staying."

He guessed right. He said he lived with his daughter, who was making hamburgers for dinner, and if I wanted to, I could join them. I accepted and soon learned that the gentleman's name was Al and that he was a professional music arranger. Later in the evening, a man came by to pick up music for his wife. He was a contractor, building navy housing. He said he would hire me as a member of a cleaning crew; the money was quite good at $2 an hour. If I wanted the job he would arrange for me to be picked up early in the morning. I was hired.

But my new friend, Al, had other plans. He said, "You have to get out of the hotel first; it is too expensive." He said he knew a singer, for whom he worked, who was looking for a roommate. So, Al arranged for us to meet at his place the next day. Maura, which was her name, came. She was Irish, and she worked as a secretary during the day and as a singer at night. She checked me out and said, "Get yourself a mattress and move in". I have forgotten all the details of how we went about getting what I needed, but the next day I moved in with Maura, and I also started to work cleaning navy housing. This suburb was near Tripler Hospital.

I would stand at the corner at 5:00 AM on Kalakaua Avenue and wait for my ride. I found this all very interesting. The Hawaiian ladies were very nice to me. They shared their food, which sometimes consisted of steamed rice and raw tuna, with a mango for dessert. It was all so different. I tried hard to fit in. The money was actually quite good. I earned enough to pay my share of the rent and could support myself.

Maura had a girlfriend, Chris, who worked as the chef's secretary for the Halekulani's top hotel manager. The Halekulani was, and still is, the first hotel in town. These two ladies decided that I could do better than working as a cleaning woman for a housing project. I should at least be a waitress at the hotel. Chris arranged an appointment for me with her big boss. Maura had helped me fill out an application. She told me how to spell waitress and whatever else I needed to know to fill in the blanks. Well, I was hired, not yet as a waitress, but as a boss girl, which meant cleaning the tables and getting the supplies from the main kitchen for the coffee shop.

I quit my cleaning job but saw my former working companions on the beach every now and then. At that time, Hawaii was still very much the old Hawaii. Natives still occupied the beach playing the ukulele. I did the best I could at all my jobs, and it did not take too long until I started to work as a waitress. My English was still pretty bad, but the Hawaiian people spoke pidgin English, which was different from the American English, but not much better than mine.

This is where I met my husband, but that is another story. I'd like to write Walter's story first and then our lives together.

Biographical sketch of Walter Brand, my husband

Walter was the youngest of four children. His father, William Brand, was born on June 12, 1897. His mother, Cecilia Maria Brand, was born on December 11, 1897. Walter's mother had two miscarriages besides the four live births. Albert was the twin of Gertrud, their only girl in the family. Walter's twin, who was also a boy, was stillborn when his mother was five months pregnant. Walter was born prematurely and was placed in an incubator. Walter's life was a struggle from the beginning and it continued to be through his early childhood. "He was slow in learning how to speak," his mother said, "but he made up for it later."

Walter's oldest brother, Helmut, was born August 21, 1925, and his other brother, Werner, on July 30, 1931. Then, Gertrud came, a joy to their mother and father. Walter, who was the youngest, was born November 1, 1932.

Gertrud passed away at the age of ten of pneumonia. We still have a little, fancy porcelain cup and saucer which Gertrud had received as a gift at her first communion. Walter mentioned that he remembered seeing Gertrud laid out in her casket in the living-room.

Walter was born in the heart of Dortmund, an industrial city that was also known for its breweries. In fact, Walter's father worked in the office of the Union Brewery practically his entire adult life. He had lost his right leg in the First World War and was severely handicapped.

Walter remembered how his father had difficulty walking and needed a cane. The streetcar that he took to go to work was a couple of blocks from their house. In winter, when the streets were wet and slippery, his mother would take him, and this big man had to lean on the frail women for support. Walter told us how he had to take his dad's wooden leg to the repairman for relining, etc.

Sometime during Walter's early childhood the family moved to Koerne, a suburb of Dortmund. Here they lived in a townhouse, which had three bedrooms, a living room and kitchen, and a basement for storage and for drying clothes. In the back of the house they had a fairly large garden, where they had a pear, cherry, and apple tree besides growing gooseberries and currants, potatoes, and all kinds of vegetables. Walter often talked about how he was the son who helped his mother working the garden. I believe this to be true, because Walter was always ready to lend a helping hand throughout all the years we were married.

He went to kindergarten in the neighborhood at the Libori Parish. He entered school at the age of six. Holidays were often spent at their grandparents' house on their father's side. On Sunday afternoons they sometimes went for long walks. Father would take the streetcar to an outdoor restaurant, where they bought a soft drink for the kids; dad had his beer and mom her cup of coffee. Cake was brought from home.

World War II started a short time after this blissful time in 1939. Mother Brand was ordered to work in an office for the Wehrmacht. Food was getting rationed, and bombing raids became more frequent, especially in the industrial part of Germany in which Walter grew up. At the age of ten, Walter was evacuated to a relative in the countryside, near Padaborn. Most children were taken out of the big industrial cities for security reasons. Helmut, at the age of seventeen was drafted into the navy. His brother, Werner, went someplace near the Black Forest.

Walter actually liked the life on the farm with all the animals; besides, his relatives had a small grocery store, a restaurant, bar, and the post office; all of it under one roof. It was a busy place, since the able-bodied men were fighting the war. Walter learned to milk the cows, work the fields, bring lunch to the farm-help, and drive the cows home at night. He worked and ate with the Polish and Russian prisoners of war, side by side. All ate at the same large family table, even though this was verboten (forbidden) by the government.

In 1945, when the war was over, he wanted nothing more than to go home, hoping that his family was still alive. The train tracks were bombed, so he started to walk home about seventy kilometers. From time to time he would catch a ride on a horse-pulled milk cart. Walter could hardly recognize his home because it was so badly damaged by the bombs. He did find his parents inside, thank God. Soon, Werner came home; he too had walked and hitchhiked all the way from southern Germany.

Helmut, the sailor, was stationed at the Baltic Sea. He too came home but much later. Living space was scarce and so was food. Walter was now thirteen years old. He shared not only the parent's bedroom, but even the bed.

Schools were either bombed or occupied by Allied soldiers. Walter's parents tried to find an apprenticeship for him in a bakery. At the beginning of the war, Walter had spent a couple of weeks in the Sauerland with relatives who owned a bakery. He had expressed a wish to learn the baker's trade. This fit into the parents' program, since they wondered how to feed three growing boys with the little food that was available.

Food was hard to come by, and people would plunder the fields for food before the potatoes or whatever else the farmer tried to grow was ready for harvest. Walter landed an apprenticeship at Dahlman's bakery, which in 2006 celebrated its one hundredth anniversary. He had room and board and learned the baker's trade. Much of the time was spent with all kinds of work that had nothing to do with baking. This would include babysitting, shoveling coal into the basement, and shoveling snow in the winter, as well as turning the soil in the garden to grow vegetables, etc. Even for the bakery, the flour and other ingredients were rationed. Walter was treated as a family member, which in later years I saw was quite obvious. Every time we visited Dortmund, we had to go to Dahlman's Bakery. Even after Walter's master and the lady of the house had passed away and the son had taken over the business, we stopped there and were fussed over. We had to stay for coffee and cake or sandwiches.

"Walter was a hard worker, dependable and totally honest," they said. After three years of learning how to make different kinds of bread and cakes, the situation in Germany had not improved enough to secure a good job. Walter went on to another master to learn how to be a pastry and sugar baker, which we call Konditor.

He added 2-½ more years to his apprenticeship. Again he had room and board, and on weekends he went home on a bike with a suitcase full of dirty laundry for his mother to wash.

Werner had learned how to be an electrician and Helmut completed an apprenticeship as a grocery salesman. Father Brand worked in an office in the Union Brewery, and mom worked hard keeping the household afloat, dividing her time between shopping, (carrying everything from the streetcar to the house), cooking, cleaning, and gardening. The weekends were spent doing piles of laundry and ironing. Father and Helmut needed white shirts for work, Werner had a blue uniform, and Walter wore black and white checkered pants and white aprons. All of it was soiled pretty badly, since clothes were not changed as frequently as is customary now.

Father Brand would help peel the potatoes and clean the vegetables, etc., but the big burden was on the mother.

Well, after Walter had completed his second apprenticeship he was ready to face the world. After all, he had two journeyman certificates in his pocket. He went to work in Duesseldorf, at the Café Kranzler. He worked there for a few months but then went on to Goeppingen to work in a Konditorei (pastry shop) there.

It was not unusual for young men to change jobs often, learning more skills along the way. From Goeppingen, Walter went on to Switzerland. He worked a season in the French part and later worked in the Italian part of Switzerland, in Ascona, at Lake Maggiore.

I like to relate an incident that happened some fifteen years later. We were traveling with our boys in Switzerland when Walter wanted to show us where he had worked. We entered a coffee house in Ascona. Walter had told us he would not make himself known because many years had passed, and he had only worked there for one season. We sat down and ordered a coffee and some pastries for the four of us. The man behind the counter kept looking at us. Walter whispered to me, "He is the boss." All of a sudden the man comes toward us and says, "Brand, Brand beer?" We did not know what he was talking about. He shook Walter's hand and said he had just ordered Brand Bier from Holland. When it was recommended to him he thought of Walter, and since he had been a decent worker, the beer by the same name could not be bad, so he had ordered it. The fact that he even remembered Walter was, of course, a pleasant surprise. He picked up the bill and talked for a while, and we were on our way to take a boat ride on Lake Maggiore.

Walter liked Switzerland as a country and also as a place to work. He worked most of his time at the Café Zimmermann, in St. Gallen, where he had a chance to learn new skills and how to make different kinds of pastries, candies, and ice creams. He joined the men's choir and developed lifelong friendships. St. Gallen is a beautiful city with a grand cathedral and a world-renowned ancient library, which he was eager to show us.

It was in St. Gallen that he applied for a position to work for the European Olympic team in Australia. The year was 1956. Walter was hired and after a short trip home to Dortmund to say good-bye, he took the train to Genoa, Italy, where on October 9, 1956, he boarded a ship by the name Flaminia. This was the last ship passing through the Suez

Canal before it was closed on account of the war between Israel and Egypt.

On the ship he met people from different parts of Europe who were hired to work for the Olympiad. Among them were John from Holland, a chef, and his Swiss wife, Trudy, who would work as a waitress. They became lifelong friends and even after John had passed away and Trudy had remarried they stayed in touch. In fact, Trudy and her new husband came to visit us in California in 1998, some forty-plus years later.

They worked in Melbourne during the Olympics and met and shook hands with Prince Phillip of Great Brittan and other dignitaries. Walter learned to adjust in a multinational and multicultural environment. Once the Games were over, Walter and most Europeans who had been hired for the event had committed themselves to stay for three years and help to get this under populated continent on its feet. Walter, John, and Trudy went to work at the Wrest Point Hotel in Hobart on the island of Tasmania.

Walter said that he often felt lonely, especially on Sundays when all the public places were closed in Australia. He was grateful to John and Trudy, who always made him feel at home.

After his three years were completed he had saved enough money to take the long journey back to Europe. He took the Flaminia to Honolulu; from there he flew to San Francisco, and took the Greyhound bus cross country to New York, via Las Vegas, Salt Lake City, and Washington D.C. Walter loved photography and took many pictures of his journey.

In New York he boarded the *Bremen* to go back to Germany to see his family. From there, he went back to Switzerland, where he started again at his old job at Zimmermann's in St. Gallen.

On the *Bremen*, which was a passenger ship, he had met a lady named Wera, who had emigrated from Prague to Canada but was now living in Honolulu. This lady was married to an Air Force officer in Hawaii. Wera was on a trip back to Europe to visit her mother. She had promised Walter she would help him find a sponsor for him so he could immigrate to the USA. Lo and behold, after a few months back in Europe news came that he could go to the American embassy and apply for a visa to immigrate to the United States.

Wow, this was good news, he thought. Things started to happen fast. Within a few weeks, he again went home to see his parents, brothers and sisters in law, and friends to say good-bye.

This time he flew all the way from Frankfurt to Honolulu, where he was welcomed like a dignitary by a welcoming committee. These men, it turned out later, were to be his fellow workers.

They had brought the traditional flower leis to hang around his neck, covering part of his three-piece, dark blue, woolen suit, which had taken him some time to save up for, but was not necessarily the outfit to wear in Hawaii.

He was led to a hut, made of corrugated metal, which was going to be his home for the near future. The front part of the hut served as bakeshop. The next day, he was asked to make apple pie. Poor Walter; he had never heard of apple pie. Luckily, these fellow workers helped him out. They learned from each other; their creations sold very well.

Walter earned some money and started to save up for a Vespa or some other type of motor scooter. He realized Hickam Air Force Base was located at the end of the world, or so it seemed. He needed some form of transportation to get to Honolulu and to Waikiki.

Honolulu, where our lives together started

Working at the Halekulani Coffee Shop at the beach of Waikiki, I passed by the large table in the corner and heard people speaking German. I could not figure it out. Where did they come from, and what were they doing here? Besides, they gave the impression they were well off. Walter was among them. I proceeded to give them water, like it was my job to do as a busgirl. I asked them where they were from. Walter answered, "Westphalia, Germany." Wow! That is where I came from. We exchanged a few words and then Walter said, "Since we are from the same area, we ought to meet later and talk." I let him know that I would start working as a waitress the next day, and that I would have to learn much and would have no time. If he wanted to see me, it would have to be this very evening, and that I would get off work at 6:00 pm.

Well, 6:00 pm came, and Walter was there with his scooter. He invited me into a drugstore coffee shop on Kalakauer Avenue. As we entered he said, "If you order anything more than a hamburger and Coke you will have to pay for it. I am broke." Boy, that guy has some nerve, I thought. Walter came back the next day. He helped me clean up the coffee shop, put the chairs on the tables, and hose the beach sand off the floor.

It did not take long before he found himself a small, furnished apartment in Honolulu. He would come around to Maura's and my place. Maura, who was ten years older than me, saw potential that I was not aware of.

She kept on saying, "Maria, he is from the same area as you are, he has good credentials, is honest, and, besides, he is good looking, even though he is somewhat on the heavy side". She was right, he had beautiful brown eyes and thick, dark, curly hair. I did like him a lot, but what bothered me was that he would come over to our place after work, empty the coffee can, where I kept my tips, and start to count my money. He had borrowed money from me already, brought his dirty shirts over for me to wash, and felt very much at home at Maura's and my place.

One day, Maura appeared in the coffee-shop and informed me that the owner of our apartment had given us official notice to move out. Maura said she would move in with a lady she worked with. Now, what was I going to do? Walter came to pick me up after work like he did whenever he could. When I told him about my predicament, he said, "Come over to my place so we can talk about it."

He took something out of his makeshift desk and handed it to me. It was some paper folded in a square and taped with scotch tape. He said, "Open it." That was easier said than done. I struggled to get it open without tearing it. It said, "Marry Maria, February 1961." I was stunned. He watched me and then said, "I want to marry you, but I am stuck in this contract and do not make enough money to offer you what you deserve. In fact, I already owe you $300. What do you say? Let's get married. This apartment is big enough for the two of us. We both get our meals at work, and we earn enough to pay for the rest."

This all was much too fast for me. I thought of what Maura had said. I remembered that my father wondered if I would ever think of marriage. I said yes but told him that I would like to get married in a church and that he would have to write to my parents and get their OK also.

We agreed, and basically both of us where relieved and happy to have made that decision. We started planning our wedding. The German ladies that Walter had met on the beach were very willing to help me buy the dress. Walter bought a white tuxedo, not believing in renting one, which is customary in America but seemed to us as starting off on the wrong foot.

Walter and I both wrote home informing our parents of our plans. Both sets of parents wrote back that we had decided too quickly. We should give it more time. To assure them that we were serious, we suggested that Walter's parents visit my parents, since Werner, Walter's brother, had a car and could drive his parents to Vreden, my hometown.

All went well, and both parents felt that we came from a good and stable family. I was told later that my father-in-law, who had lost his right leg in the First World War and walked with a cane, had walked around my parents' house, inspected the building, and said something like, "Hmm, a brick building, very sturdy. I think it is OK for them to marry." This struck me as funny, that a decision like marriage could be based on the sturdiness of a brick building.

Anyway, we both got the approval of our parents, which was nice to have, but would not have changed our minds anyway.

So, on the first of October, 1960, we were married in the Sacred Heart Church on Wilder Avenue in Honolulu, Hawaii. We had a lovely wedding, even though we had only my brother present as a family member. He was the best man, and Hildegund, since she was a Catholic, was the maid of honor.

Hildegund was already widowed with two children. She had married a Hawaiian GI after the war, as had the other German ladies that Walter had met at the Waikiki beach. They all met on Sunday afternoons for a get-together. All of them came to our rescue. Two German brothers, who had immigrated to Hawaii and operated a carpet business, drove us to church in their car. Maura, who entertained the guests at the hotels on weekend evenings, sang the "Ave Maria" for us at the ceremony. Johanna, who was a buyer at the Liberty House, went with me to buy the wedding dress, and Al, who had helped me out that first evening in Honolulu when I was lost and to whom I owed much, gave me away as a father figure. Walter's fellow workers helped to make the wedding cake. The people I worked with had collected money and gave us a set of dishes. Everyone was more than accommodating and most of them came to the wedding.

Our reception was at the Ranch House, where Walter knew a Swiss cook. We had cordon blue as a main course. It was a very special day, and we even went on a honeymoon to the island of Kauai.

We stayed at the Coco Palm Hotel, which was affiliated with the Halekulani Hotel. The hotel arranged a tour for all the honeymooners and took us to the Grand Canyon of the Pacific and to the Fern Grotto, where a Hawaiian lady in her native dress sang the "Hawaiian Wedding Song." These are lovely memories.

We somehow managed to pay for it all.

Back in Honolulu, we continued our work, lived in our apartment, which was quite cozy, invited some friends over for potato pancakes, etc.

Our scooter served us well. We rode all over the island, stopped at the pineapple fields, ate mangos that had fallen off the trees, and went to the local markets to buy all the tropical fruit we would want.

I remember that on Christmas Eve, I worked in the main dining room of the hotel. The room was grand in the Hawaiian style, with huge lava rocks and water features, beautifully decorated with all kinds of orchids and tropical plants. The band played "Stille Nacht" (Silent Night). My thoughts wandered home, and I struggled not to cry.

Walter and I had bought a small but real Christmas tree. These were shipped over from the mainland. We placed it on a wooden egg crate that I had covered with a pillowcase cover. A few bulbs from Woolworth dime store finished off our first Christmas tree.

A few months later, Walter had completed his contract. We started making plans to go back to the mainland. Walter was sure that he could land a good job in a hotel and that we could make a good living in San Francisco, the city both of us had been to and both of us liked.

We shipped our few belongings, including the scooter, off to San Francisco, said good-bye to our friends and to Honolulu, boarded a plane, and off we went. We took the train to Chicago and Milwaukee. I felt sick to my stomach. Motion sickness, I thought, but after a while I suspected I was pregnant. Our Roelfchen was our precious souvenir from Hawaii.

We visited my brother and friends in Milwaukee, and even gave a party to celebrate our wedding. Then again we packed a few items, including my electric sewing machine, stayed for a few days, and flew back to San Francisco.

We stayed at a small hotel downtown, where we experienced our first earthquake. It was quite scary when the bed moved back and forth in the room and people in their nightgowns huddled in the hallways.

We decided to stay in San Francisco and started to look for an apartment. We moved in at 395 Twenty-fifth Avenue, at the corner of Clement Street.

Walter landed a job at the Mark Hopkins Hotel, one of the best hotels in San Francisco. I tried to find a job as a waitress, but when the owners found out I was pregnant, they did not hire me. Yet, luck was on our side. The owner of the apartment house asked me to manage the building. I had no experience but said I would give it a good try.

Ralph, our oldest son, was born November 12, 1961

Neither one of us had experience with children, but we figured we would manage OK. I took a class, which the doctor had recommended, to learn how to hold a baby, change diapers, etc. We bought a crib and some baby clothes. Walter had started a new job as a pastry cook at United Airlines, making desserts for first-class passengers. He worked the afternoon shift. I cleaned and rented the apartments. We saved on rent and were paid $15 extra for cleaning a vacant unit. This would pay for a week's groceries. All apartments were furnished, including ours. I called the style Salvation Army antique. Competition was tough. Every block had "For Rent" signs in the window. I tried to keep the mailboxes polished, flowers on the table in the entry hall, and the staircase vacuumed and dusted. At times I would buy remnants and sew curtains, etc., in order to make the apartments more appealing to prospective tenants.

The apartments were located at a busy street where buses stopped at all four corners. This was good for the rental business, but it was also noisy.

It was the first home for our Roelfchen, (German for Ralph). He was born on a Sunday morning, November 12, 1961, at St. Mary's Hospital in San Francisco. We were so happy to have him. At the time, fathers were not present in the delivery room, but when Walter walked into my room, I could tell he was very pleased. We paid for all the expenses ourselves. The insurance did not consider having a baby a sickness, and, therefore, this was not covered. We had saved up for this, and when I left the hospital two days later, we paid the bill in full.

Walter drove up with his new Comet, (the scooter had served as a down payment) and packed our baby and me into the front seat and drove to our home on Twenty-fifth Avenue.

Walter helped us onto the sidewalk but then had to hurry to go to work. He had started at United Airlines on June 21, 1961. He did not dare ask for a day off, and he was late for work as it was.

I took my Roelfchen and my bag and walked up the stairs to our tiny apartment. On the kitchen table was a beautifully decorated cake. The writing on it said, "Welcome home, Mama and Ralph."

That was Walter for you, always thinking of doing something special for us. I was happy. In the afternoon, Inge, a German lady I had met at work, came over to help me take care of Roelfchen. Things went pretty good. The doctor even came by the house to see how I was doing. I do not know why, but the doctor advised against breastfeeding. So our baby started out with formula. Walter helped with feeding, changing, and rocking the baby to sleep. He would even go to the launderette across the street with the diaper pail, as a matter of fact, just as I did.

Ralph was baptized in Santa Monica Church on Geary Boulevard. We were dressed up for the occasion. Walter wore his dark suit, and I had my new pink pillbox hat to show off.

We had invited a few friends. In church, Ralph started screaming. Walter whipped out the bottle of formula from his side pocked, all wrapped in a towel to keep it warm. I had not thought of bringing one, but Walter did.

I like to explain why we named our first baby Rolf (Ralph).

When I did housework in Stuttgart, their three-year-old son, Rolf, was with me much of the time, helping me go shopping, cooking, cleaning, and delivering meat products to the customers. I had never been much around young children before and did not really know what to do with them. This little boy made me realize that he was already a whole person who would try to manipulate me, make me do things for him he could easily do for himself, etc. He was a very loving little boy, and we became the best of friends. I would even volunteer to take him with me on my day off. In other words, he taught me to love children. Since Walter did not really care to have a Walter the second, I asked him if we could call our first baby boy, Rolf. Walter agreed, and Rolf it was, which to my surprise turned into Ralph.

Walter's Swiss friend Monty and his wife, whom Walter had met and spent much time with in Australia, now lived in Stockton, California, and they were the godparents. We celebrated in our tiny apartment, and we made it as festive as we could.

There were many precious moments, and I'd like to share a couple. I had started a new bottle with a new nipple. I fed Ralph almost every hour. He would suck on that nipple, give up after a while and go back to sleep, just to wake up a short while later crying. I would start the whole process all over again. It was a cold night, and Walter was at work. I picked Ralph up and looked at him in despair and frustration, just to have him smile at me and give me a mischievous look. I calmed down; looking at this sweet little face thinking he already is playing tricks on me. I inspected the nipple on the bottle and realized the hole was just too tiny. There was no way he could draw the formula through it. I got a needle, held it over the flame and enlarged the hole in the nipple. After this, my Roelfchen could drink, and his little tummy finally found satisfaction. He went to sleep in my arms. I laid him in the crib, and he slept for hours. I will never forget the look on that little face.

We had a good life, the three of us, but after a couple of months I started looking for a job. Walter worked a rotating shift and had different days off every week. It turned out we needed a babysitter only every sixth week for two days. All the other times, one of us was home taking care of our baby. Our neighbor next door had already offered to baby-sit on those days. She was from Ireland; her husband was from France. They had two little girls, and she looked forward to earning a few extra dollars.

Ralph was quite happy there. One day, he was about six months old, I picked him up. He was all flush and made happy grunts. He had sand in his booty, and his little toe was poking through a hole. He looked so cute, a real boy, I thought. This was when I really hugged and cuddled him. These are precious memories, and there are many more.

We had our first Christmas as a complete family. Money was scare, but we had everything we needed. I made a cute little outfit for Ralph, knitted a sweater for Walter, and bought a toaster for our family. I don't even remember what I got. Inge, who had become part of the family, and a couple of other German ladies she knew, came to celebrate with us. These ladies worked in an office, rented a room, and shared a kitchen. We had at least an apartment, and so they came to us.

We all enjoyed singing, and much of the time was spent eating and singing or playing a game. In the afternoon all of us went for a walk. Ralph received plenty of attention. It was a good way to spend a holy day.

So it was; life went on. I worked part time as a waitress and kept up the apartments.

Walter learned from the landlord how to fix things but did not get paid extra for it. The landlord would say, "Walter, what I teach you now will make money for you the rest of your life." After he left, we would say, "Yes, this is all well and good, but we need the money now." The landlord taught us much, and I have to admit, he was right.

First trip to Germany; my father died

In November of 1962, Ralph and I flew to Germany. I had not been home for more than six years and since my family in Germany had no telephone, I had not spoken to them either. Walter had been working at United Airlines and was entitled to a free flight after working for them for one year. We took advantage of that privilege. I was happy to show off my baby, who was a chubby little boy. Besides, my father was very ill, and I longed to see him and the rest of my family. Walter arrived in Germany a couple of weeks later. Ralph and I landed in Duesseldorf. My father and one of my cousins came to the airport to take us home. Walter's father and mother were also on hand to welcome us. This was the first time I saw my in-laws in person. Ralph screamed at the top of his lungs. There was nothing I could do to calm him down. We stopped at the airport restaurant for a bite to eat and to get acquainted. Oma (Grandmother) Brand was able to make Ralph feel at ease. He was tired and out of his routine. I was shocked to see how old my father looked.

My parents had borrowed a crib for Ralph. In the late afternoon, my father would heat a brick in the oven, wrap it in a towel, and place it in the crib to make it nice and warm. Ralph could not walk yet. He made his first steps in my parents' house with my father and mother spending time to teach him.

When Walter came, we had a party at my parents' house and celebrated our wedding. We had plenty of Wurst (sausage), potato salad, and other goodies. There was beer and schnapps. People even danced in the kitchen, and the men smoked heavily. (In our area women seldom smoked.) It was a good time. My cousins from next door took part, and my sisters and their families were all present.

A couple of days later, my father took me to the jewelry store. He said that I had never cost them any money and that he wanted to buy me something special. I was thrilled, and I chose a golden arm bangle which I still treasure.

I also was given my inheritance. The largest one of the three pigs in the pigsty was sold, and the money was mine to spend freely. I decided to buy bone china with the money, and it covered the cost for a twelve-place settings; twelve coffee service, platters, bowls, etc. It all was shipped to our apartment in San Francisco. We had no chair nor bed to call our own, but I had a set of Thierschenreuter china, fit for a king.

A few days later we went to see Walter's family in Dortmund. It was time to say good-bye to Vreden. Walter's parents and brothers and their families went out of their way to show us a good time. All of them fussed over Ralph like my family had done. Ralph also found a playmate in Susanne, his cousin, who was a little older than Ralph.

Oma Brand's birthday was coming up on December 11. There was supposed to be a party a couple of days earlier, because we were scheduled to fly back to America on December 11.

About noon, the phone at my in-laws rang. It was my oldest brother. His voice was very somber. He informed me that father was dying, and since we were still in Germany, maybe we could come home once more to see my father alive.

We rented a car, and off to Vreden we went. We stopped the car in front of our house. My youngest sister moved the curtain away from the window to look out. She was crying as dad was inside the house, lying on his bed, dying. I had lived through this very scene many times in a recurring dream. It was strange.

We went inside the house. My father was conscious. His circulation had gone haywire. The doctor gave him just a couple more hours to live.

Since Walter had the car, he was sent to get my father's brother, who lived at the homestead. All sat in the kitchen praying the rosary. My father called me and said, "Marieken, (that was his name for me) go back to America. Stick to your husband and take care of your family. Never mind what might happen here." I cried. We said good-bye, and Walter and I went back to Dortmund and the next day back to America. Our Ralph could walk now, and he was busy running around at the airport.

We celebrated Christmas in our tiny apartment. It was cozy. We had a Christmas tree, using the same bulbs we had used in Hawaii. Ralph wore the cute outfit I had made for him. Walter had to work on Christmas day, but when he came home that night we had a nice dinner and celebrated in a quiet but very nice way.

We bought our first property, a duplex, May 1, 1964

In the spring the landlord offered us a two-bedroom apartment on the first floor. After a couple of years we started to acquire property ourselves and bought a converted duplex for $29,000. We both applied what we had learned as an apartment house manager.

This house was old and needed fixing up. It was in a good location, had a great view, and had a large backyard. In other words, it had great potential.

Walter painted, wallpapered, changed water heaters and stoves. I did much of the prep work and cleaned the yard. Ralph helped me. He collected snails into a coffee can. Ralph was a good toddler, always happy and eager to help.

When it was time to go home, we would either buy an ice cream cone and walk home or take the bus and share a piece of gum. Every penny was saved.

We sold this duplex after six months of ownership. This was the least amount of time one had to keep property in order to take advantage of a tax benefit. We had invested $3,000 as a down payment, $2,000 to fix it up, and made a couple thousand on the sale. We now had $7,000 cash and invested it into on old Victorian, four-unit apartment house in the Richmond district in San Francisco. Again this was a fixer-upper. Walter seemed to thrive on making old buildings look good again. We spent most of our free time working on our apartments, or I was cleaning the apartments we managed and renting them. I could never understand why American people moved so frequently. This was totally foreign to us.

We tried hard to keep the places rented and did not lose a day's rent during these years. We worked hard; one of us worked the late shift while the other had the early shift. We wrote each other notes that went something like this: Ralph ate all his Mittagessen (midday meal, main meal for us); he had a good nap. I took him to the hardware store and then stopped for an ice cream. See you later, Dad.

When I had a chance I would take Ralph to the playground. There I met other mothers or grandmothers with little children, and Ralph had a couple of children to play with.

We had few friends because we had little free time and worked odd hours. I began to feel sick to my stomach, a sure sign I was pregnant again.

I kept on working for a while, until my condition became too obvious.

Second trip to Germany; Walter's father died

We received notice from Walter's family that his father had cancer on his bronchial tubes. This was bad news. Again we flew home, all three of us. We visited with his father in the hospital, who was deathly ill. On one of those visits, Opa Brand stripped the gold watch off his hand and gave it to Ralph, saying that he had no use for it any longer and that he wanted Ralph, his only grandson, to have it.

We were visiting my family when we received word that my father-in-law, Wilhelm Brand, at age sixty-seven, had passed away. It was Christmas eve 1964. We went back to Dortmund to be with Walter's mother, brothers, and sisters-in-law. We spent the Christmas holidays together.

Opa Brand had a nice funeral. The choir, of which he had been a member for more than fifty years, sang at his graveside.

After a few days, Ralph and Oma were getting along so well, Walter decided we should go to Switzerland for a few days to see his friends. Switzerland was beautiful in winter. His friends treated us well, but then it was time to go back to Dortmund.

When we entered the house Ralph screamed and ran past me to Walter. He had missed him so much. I felt hurt and guilty. Why would he go to dad and pass me by? In general, Roelfchen had spent more time with dad than with me. I worked the day shift and was with him only after 4:00 PM When our four-plex or the apartments we managed had a vacancy, I was the one who rented them because people would come after work to look at the place. I was busy, suffered from modern mom syndrome.

But Ralph was only three years old, and it was wrong of us to have left him in a strange house. Oma, though, said that they had had a good time together and that it had been good for her to take care of him after all the upset with Opa passing away, etc.

I was getting bigger and could not work as a waitress any longer. The boss at the Fairmont Hotel, where I worked the breakfast and lunch shift in the main dining room, assured me I could work there again after the baby was born. The earnings had been good, and there were times that I earned more than Walter.

Walter used the money I earned to fix up the apartments. He had never done this type of work before, but he was quick to learn and did a good job. We increased the rents, which also brought up the value of the property.

Raymond entered our small family

It was Tuesday, May 11, 1965, when our Raymond came into this world. I was ironing the evening before and watched TV. I knew something was happening and hoped Walter would get home on time from work, which he did. After midnight he took me to the hospital. He stayed with me until I went into the delivery room. Then he went to take the car out of the emergency area, and when he came back the doctor met him in the hallway and congratulated him on the new son. He came out so fast. I had heard the women moaning and groaning in the labor room, and was sure that I would be one of them soon, when, before I knew it, everything was behind me.

The baby was born with a sore on his nose. He had been very active in my stomach and probably hurt himself trying to get out.

Walter came into my room and said, "Another boy; that is fine, it might be more economical in the long run." Walter had brought the camera and took some pictures. Raymond was born at Kaiser Hospital on Geary Boulevard in San Francisco. I was in the hospital two nights. On the third day I was released. The insurance paid for it this time.

Walter took me with my bundle of joy to the car, where Ralph had been waiting. He was not allowed to come inside the hospital, but he was a good boy and waited patiently for us. He was so eager to see his little brother. We let him hold him and stroke him. We went home to our apartment. Once again a cake was waiting there for us, and this time Walter was able to stay with us and not go to work.

We were a happy family even though we still had no chair to call our own. I made time available to take the boys to the playground whenever I could. Ralph had always been so quiet and mostly played in the sandbox, but now he took it upon himself to protect his little brother when he thought other kids were getting too close. Ralph had made a few friends and looked forward to playing with them. I invited them and their mothers to our apartment on a rainy day for some hot chocolate and cookies.

Below our apartment, on the ground floor, was a fur store, and to keep the kids from running around I would read them a story. One day, Ralph said, "Mom, don't read a story; they just laugh at you afterwards." It made me aware that I had an accent, and that it was embarrassing for Ralph. That is the burden of immigrant children.

Walter and I kept on working and saving our money. The boys were developing nicely. Ray was a little more difficult than Ralph had been. Ralph would just about eat anything, be it spinach or oatmeal. Ray would take it in his mouth and then spit it out all over the place. Once, on the playground, I was struggling to feed him, and a grandma, who was there with her grandson, said, "I wanted to go home some time ago, but I want to see who is winning this game, you or your son." He would fight me all the way. Even changing a diaper was a challenge. He would wiggle around so much that I had to lay him on the floor and hold him down to change him.

Ralph at times was a little jealous. He too would lie down on the floor beside Ray and want to be changed as well.

Walter found a toy box in the garbage area that had been discarded by one of the tenants. He brought it inside, glued it together again, painted it, and wrote the boys' names on top. When we showed it to them, and Ralph realized that his name was shorter than Raymond's, he objected and wanted the names reversed. Oh, what we can learn about human nature by studying our own children.

On the weekends, when Walter worked, I would take them to church and go to Golden Gate Park later to play in the sandbox or on the swings.

We loved them both, but I was not used to showing it so openly. In Westphalia, where we grew up, hugging and kissing was not done publicly. Years later when I went to visit my family, I noticed my sisters smooching with their children. I became aware of how things had changed. We always knew that our parents loved and protected us, yet it was not so obvious. "I love you" was not being said in so many words, not even from husband to wife or vice versa. I found this lovey-dovey business was greatly exaggerated in America and not sincere, or so it seemed to me.

Raymond took his time to learn how to speak. Ralph would do it for him. "Raymond will was zu trinken haben" he would say, which translates to, "Raymond wants something to drink."

One day I read in the newspaper that the USS Enterprise, a big Navy ship, would anchor in San Francisco. It was my day off, and I took the boys to the Sea Cliff Beach to watch the ship sail under the Golden Gate. We were having a picnic when Ray said, "Big boat." I was surprised and happy; he had said something without me making him.

In 1966 we bought the duplex on Twenty-sixth Avenue

On January 22, 1966, we had the four-unit apartment house refinanced and bought the duplex on Twenty-sixth Avenue, near the Russian church. We told our landlord we would move out but had another German couple lined up who would be happy to take our position and manage his apartments for him. He agreed.

We moved into our new (for us it was new) property. We rented out the upstairs. In the back of our house was a good-sized yard, which, at the end, had a cozy one-room apartment. Inge, our friend, who had rented a room in the city and shared a kitchen with a few other people, was eager to fix this garden apartment up and move in. We helped her and paid for the expense.

Then, something happened. United Airlines went on strike. At the same time, San Francisco got a new tax assessor. All property was reevaluated and taxes shot up. Our properties did not support themselves any longer. We had to pay out of our pockets. I was not working, and Walter was on strike. The bathtub upstairs had a leak, and neither we nor the tenants knew it. One day the ceiling in our downstairs bathroom caved in.

We needed money, and fast. I went to look for work. It seemed that all the wives of the United Airlines mechanics were looking for waitress jobs. I landed a job as a carhop at Otts Restaurant at Fisherman's Warf from 10:00 PM until 7:00 AM. This was a place where the bartenders and people who cater to the nightlife would hang out. It was a good experience, and I learned to respect these people, whom I had somewhat looked down upon before.

Walter got a part-time job at David's Deli and Bakery. Inge had to jump in and baby-sit sometimes.

Soon, the strike was over. Walter went back to work, and I found myself a better job. Again we worked different shifts. When I think about it now, I wonder how we did it.

Oma Brand came to visit on October 1, 1967. She stayed for four months. We got along well, but Oma was very conscious of what people might say and mentioned I should dress better. I still had an old coat from Germany. She did not realize that it takes time and sacrifice to make that seed money.

At another time Ray and Oma were gone, and it was getting dark. Walter and I started out in different directions looking for them. Ralph had instructions to stay home. When he saw Oma and Ray come toward the house, he opened the window and said, "Oma, Papa is ganz unverschaemt of you," meaning, "Papa is very angry with you," but he said it in half German and English in a funny way.

She would take the boys to Ocean Beach and Ray would say, "Heiss" (hot) every time a spray of water would get them wet. Oma would help clean and cook. One day she went with a bucket outside, when Ray climbed out of his high chair, slammed the door behind her, and said, "Oma, bye, bye." He loved Oma dearly and cried so hard when he saw her walk the steps onto the airplane.

We celebrated Christmas in our sparsely furnished unit. We still had some Salvation Army antique furniture; that is what I called our style. The boys' bedroom came from the four-unit apartment complex. Tenants had left it behind when they moved. The set was complete, solid, and sturdy, but it was dirty, had cigarettes burns on the dresser, and the hinges were broken. Walter saw possibilities. He scraped all the paint off, stained the wood, and bought new hinges, and it became our boys' bedroom set for many years. It serves me now, over forty years later, as our guest room furniture.

Somehow, we achieved our goals faster than we could have ever hoped for. We worked together toward the same goals. To celebrate our achievements, we would treat the family to a big piece of pie at Marie Callender's, a coffee shop known for its good pies.

Sometimes, I felt that we had bitten off more than we could chew, and the boys did not get the attention they needed and should have had. For instance, I worked every holiday. That deprived us of celebrating like most people would, but we were good in improvising. We had no relatives to fill the void.

One time, Raymond suggested we should get a divorce. He reasoned that he would get new grandparents, who would be here, and we would have a larger family and celebrate together, and he would get more gifts. Luckily, Walter and I never entertained that thought.

Moving to Sunnyvale in 1968

Ralph had started school at Santa Monika Catholic School in San Francisco, but after a couple of years we sold the duplex and moved to Sunnyvale in the South Bay. This area was booming. The high-tech industry was born. The weather was sunny in Sunnyvale. We had enough of a down payment from our duplex with the cozy garden apartment to buy a large, brand new four-unit apartment complex. Walter rented a U-haul, a do-it-yourself moving truck, and moved our belongings to Sunnyvale.

We went back to San Francisco to get the car and the rest of our stuff among them Raymond's used tricycle. When we arrived at our new home, Ray got on his tricycle and wanted to go back home to San Francisco. He cried bitterly.

Now we faced the task of renting the apartments. How would we advertise? The back of our house faced Highway 9 (later called Sunnyvale–Saratoga Road), which at the time was not very busy. Who would see the sign in the window? The next day the prune orchard across the street was bulldozed down. Soon the street was being widened, and traffic increased rapidly. People did respond to our sign, and we started to rent the units, which were very spacious and had a large kitchen and a fireplace in the living room. We ourselves lived in the three-bedroom owners unit. Our living room furniture consisted of a used redwood garden table and a couple of benches. Most of our tenants were decent people, but we had a few over the years who vandalized the unit they lived in. One tenant cut and damaged the magnolia tree in the backyard and, on the living room wall, wrote "Damn Nazi." We also found ketchup running down the front of the cabinets. Oh, that hurt, but we remembered the words of our San Francisco landlord, who said, "He who has the last laughs is the lucky one. These people will never have what you have."

Walter and I kept reassuring each other. We tried to be good and fair to our tenants, and they were good to us.

Boys' school years—hard on them, hard on me

Ralph started Stocklmeir School. Everything was new for us. I was not familiar with the school system and did not approve of how some things were done. Ralph brought home sheets of paper with different subjects that he had worked on. To me it seemed very confusing and just paper stuff. Nothing was organized like I knew it from Germany.

I bought myself books on how to help your child in first grade, second grade, etc. My English was not good but was improving. We had concentrated on making and saving money. We did not ever want to be a burden to the state or to anyone else, for that matter. We had been very successful in that regard.

It had not occurred to me that I was expected to work with our children doing their schoolwork. That is what schools were for, we both reasoned, and besides, when would I have the time?

We spoke German at home and with most of our friends as well. Walter was an excellent provider, but insisted that, if he could make a good living as a foreigner in a foreign land, our kids should have no trouble making it in the country of their birth, where they grew up within the system. What were we paying taxes for? Education was the school's job.

I was the one who had to see the teachers. I worried and hoped for the best. If I have any regret at all, it is not having spent more time with my boys during their school years, helping them, encouraging them, praising them, and showing more understanding and patience for the situation they found themselves in.

Sure, our equity in the houses grew, but at what price? I felt overwhelmed, and at times I yelled at the boys for no reason. I am sorry, but I am happy to say that both boys became upright citizens and successful in their work, as well as in their private lives. I am very, very grateful for that.

Ralph was a robust boy, and did not need the attention Raymond needed, I thought. Raymond seemed to demand more of my time. I learned later that Ralph believed I did not love him. In fact, he once said, "I love my dad, but my mom?"

I felt hurt but could think back on a few occasions where I had been very hard on him, but also on Raymond. Ralph wanted to play baseball. He was very good at it, too. Once, he hit a grand slam, and the team moved into a higher league because of him. The whole team and the parents came to the restaurant I was working at to tell me about it. I was busy and had little time to talk to them. I was also shy and did not know what to talk to them about since I knew very little about the game, and Walter knew even less. That must have been very embarrassing for Ralph.

The coach and parents arranged a dinner for the boys and parents at the Holiday Inn. We went, and Ralph received the ball that he had hit to make the grand slam. Everyone on the team had signed it. He treasures that ball to this day.

Walter was more into soccer and listened to the German radio station to hear the results. Ralph was into American football, which he played in high school. That was another game we knew nothing about and were not interested in. In fact we went to see Ralph play once, sat on the wrong side of the bleachers, and rooted for the wrong team. Thinking about it now, this was unforgivable and must have been very painful for Ralph.

He had a bad grade in German, and that was enough to not let him play football. His grades were not getting better, and I worried about it a great deal but could not help him anymore. I have at most six years of formal education. I could get by but was in no position to help him.

Ray, in the meantime, was doing fair in school. He questioned everything. One day he was doing his homework for religious class. We were reading: God created the sun, and the rain to make things grow. He looked at me and said, "I don't like the sun; she is too hot."

Ralph was watching television when Ray asked, "Mom, does God not love the little fish?"

My reply was not reassuring enough, because he said the big fish eat the little fish, and therefore God does not love the little fish. He had made up his mind, and I could not convince him.

Ray was not so good in sports. He was very tall for his age but not very coordinated. He rarely hit the ball at the baseball game, which was so important to him. Ralph had the trophies and Ray wanted one too. So we bought one and wrote his name on it. He threw it back at us and cried.

Oh, what were we supposed to do? We were on our own. We had no relatives to ask for advice, and most of our friends were single women from German-speaking countries I had met at work.

When we grew up, parents in general did not spend much time playing games with their children. We had uncles and aunts, cousins, and lots of kids in the neighborhood to play with. I never felt deprived of attention; someone was always around we could turn to. Here, it was all up to us.

In America, it was each family for themselves. I think the family car might have had something to do with it. People lived independently of each other. We never went to the neighbors to borrow anything, and no one ever came to us. People moved often. Not being fluent in the English language was a big handicap. I had no one to blame but myself.

It surprised me at times how quickly I was called a friend. Everybody was everybody's friend, yet close friendships seldom developed.

I suffered under this system, and I realized that coming to America had its price. In retrospect, I know it was part of growing up, but growing pains are pains just the same. I learned to confront life and deal with it as it presented itself.

Raymond wanted a dog for his birthday. We agreed, and Ray and I went to the pound to get this little black mutt with a white stripe down the front of his chest. I had never seen a happier little face than that of Raymond's on that day. The name of the dog would be Stripe, that was obvious.

Stripe was worth every penny. The boys just loved him, and so did Walter and I. He was a great companion for all of us.

Raymond also had a hard time in school. Mothers were expected to be involved as helpers in the classroom and in concession stands at Saturday's baseball games. I did not feel qualified to help the teacher but would volunteer at the concession stand, selling jawbreakers (candies), and other kinds of sweets. The profit of these sales would help defray expenses for uniforms, etc. Children had at times as much as $2 to spend. Why could they not eat an apple? All this was totally against everything I believed in. Why could they not play in their ordinary clothes instead of a uniform? Why did we have to spend the money, especially when at times games where being forfeited because not enough members of a team showed up?

Being very opinionated, I dared to voice my displeasure on the subject. I believe this was to the disadvantage of my boys.

On one occasion, Ray was supposed to be in a play. He had practiced, and I had helped him. He was excited and eager to participate. I took the day off work so I could go and see him play his little part. Well, as it turned out, he was not playing his part after all. We were both disappointed.

Another time, Ray received a bad grade in English. I went to the teacher and asked what we could do. The teacher said something about Ray was not able to cut the mustard, and there was little he, as a teacher, could do about it. I asked to see the principal. After I told the principal my concern, he said that I should not worry because Ray would be an executive some day and would have a secretary to do the writing for him. I asked, "Where does the secretary learn how to write?" I had hit a nerve. The principal turned red in his face and told me to sit down. Then he said, "You grew up in a different culture, and I do not have to remind you where it got you, do I?"

Wow, he was referring to World War II. I was devastated. I went home and wondered what to do next. I talked to Walter, but he left it up to me. I came to the conclusion that Ray was not in the right environment at that school. I took him out and transferred him to another school. This meant losing his friends and having to adjust to new surroundings.

Oh, I felt for him, but still thought it was the best thing to do. He, as well as Ralph, hated school. Both looked forward to the next grade, believing the situation would improve, but, of course, it got worse.

I learned English with them and from them. That part improved as far as I was concerned, but my poor boys struggled. When I had to call the doctor for whatever ailed the boys, I looked up Doctor Spock with the dictionary next to me and hoped I could make myself understood. All of it seems harder now than I experienced it at the time.

There were times I felt sorry for myself. Here I was in America and worked my butt off; my sisters at home in Germany took care of their children and did not work out of the house. I am glad that time is past.

Our friends in San Francisco

We always had enjoyed a good time with our friends in San Francisco and still did so when they came to visit us in Sunnyvale. We often spent a couple of hours just singing all kinds of songs that entered our minds. These folk songs, operettas, church songs, children's songs, seasonal songs, and especially the Christmas songs, were uplifting and for me were a source to replenish my soul.

At other times we would discuss subjects such as happiness, justice, beauty, politics, religion, marriage, etc., and the difference between America and Germany. This was always very interesting, but at times the talks would get quite heated. We came up with the following solution. We decided to start singing, as soon as we began to attack each other instead of the subject being debated. It was a lot of fun, and we always parted on good terms.

These ladies would also baby-sit for us when Walter and I celebrated our anniversary. This was our once a year "out on the town" event. We would go to a nice restaurant for dinner. The boys looked forward to this as well because they, too, would get a special treat, and our friends would play with them and take them to the park. We are still friends fifty-plus years later.

Joining the Germania Verein in San Jose

In 1973, Walter had the opportunity to change to the day shift. Ralph was now twelve years, and Ray was eight years old. They were not babies any more, and we felt we could now start to think of ourselves a little bit more. We learned that there was a German club in San Jose. Since Walter had sung in the men's choir in Switzerland, he was happy to learn there was a German choir in San Jose. When he came home after the first choir practice he informed me that they had just started a mixed choir, and that I could go singing also. Walter and I both enjoyed singing, something we had in common but did not know when we got married. We both joined and enjoyed the singing tremendously.

The fact that there were people who shared the same interest, with whom we shared a common background, lifestyle, and language, and who had children, made us happy.

Our problem was that I worked every Sunday and holiday for several years. It prevented us from doing things together with other families. We still managed to arrange our days off to take the boys on short trips to the snow, beach, or redwoods to watch the deer and birds. We even once went to Disneyland.

Since Walter worked for the airlines, we took advantage of air travel. Walter was a good organizer. He would plan, and we did go oversees to visit our families, or go to Hawaii, to Mexico, or to visit my brother in Wisconsin.

Ralph became a teenager. Walter and I began to go out more. There was a dance every Saturday night at the Germania. The choir went to singing meets or sang at our own Germania Hall. We had made friends and were invited to their homes. We reciprocated and had parties at our house. There was always plenty of food and drink. Most of our friends were older than we were, and their children were grown, but ours still needed us.

When I think back, I realize now that we were at times selfish and did not include our boys the way we should have. Again, I cannot change that, but I certainly would do it differently the second time around. But who gets that chance?

Walter suffered a heart attack on August 8, 1977

Like I have mentioned before, at times we bit off more than we could chew. We felt we were pretty strong. Walter would say, "I can sleep when I am dead; I do not need much sleep now." Walter worked at United Airlines full time and often overtime. After work or on weekends we would work on the apartments; Saturday evening was our night out. He also smoked about forty cigarettes a day.

A brand new, freestanding house was being built for us. All of us were excited and went to the building site to ooh and ah, and we believed we had arrived and were living the American dream.

Well, it was not meant to be. Walter woke up an August 8, 1977, with a tremendous pain in his left arm. At first he believed it was from planting a hedge around the lawn at the apartments. But the pain worsened, and Ralph, who was sixteen years old and had just received his driving permit, drove us to the hospital. Help came fast at the emergency department. We waited outside, hoping for the best. Finally the doctor came out to inform us that Dad had suffered a massive heart attack and that he was still in very serious condition. He would have to stay in the hospital for several days.

Now what? We went to see him every day. The house continued being built. My cousin and her friend were about to arrive from Germany. Inge, our friend who was more like a sister, drove us to Lake Tahoe. Walter insisted that I go with them and that I show the visitors a good time, regardless. Ray went to spend two weeks with my brother and his wife in Wisconsin.

I could tell Walter was devastated. He never smoked another cigarette since that day. He loved life, and he wanted to live. He also lost weight. After twelve days in the hospital he was at home recovering for another ten weeks.

In the meantime we had our moving day. Our friends came to the rescue. All Walter had to do was, give directions of where the furniture should be placed, etc. Ralph was a great help. He was strong and helped move the heavy items. One of our friends was a truck driver and he came and moved everything that would not fit into the family car.

We settled in, but Walter was still the type A person he had always been. We changed our lifestyle. No more smoking, no more overtime, and a healthier diet. We started to walk a couple of miles a day, every day. Our Stripy, our little black dog with the white stripe down the front, would always be ready to go. I made it my priority to walk with Walter regardless what else was on the agenda. This was special time. We could reflect, get to know the neighbors, and listen to the birds.

Ralph joined the air force

Time passed quickly. Ralph was about to graduate from high school. What was he going to do? His intention was good, but his grades were not the best. There were no apprenticeship programs in America like Walter had enjoyed in Germany. Ralph loved airplanes and talked about wanting to be a pilot. His grades were not good enough. He was color-blind and could not be an airplane mechanic. Ralph was always a good and willing worker. He had earned and saved money for a Volkswagen Beetle. It was an original and was considered an antique. He paid for everything himself.

But now, he found himself at the threshold of life. What could he learn that he would enjoy? We suggested joining the air force. He agreed. We spent one more vacation together in Cancun, Mexico. I believe he enjoyed it.

And so the time came that we brought our Ralph to Oakland on an August morning to join the air force. He was seventeen years old. Somehow we hoped that he would come back home after four years of service and go to college. He was a smart young man; all he needed was some common sense and self-confidence. We hoped the air force would teach him both.

After his basic training in Texas, he was on his way to the East Coast, where we visited him. It seemed strange; Ralph was driving and Walter sat next to him and I sat in the back seat. Our Ralph had grown up; he was in the driver's seat. Not much later, he was stationed in England.

We received letters from countries such as Egypt and other foreign places. He earned certificates of merit for outstanding work, etc.

The biggest surprise came on Walter's fiftieth birthday. Ralph called to congratulate his father and inform him that he was engaged. The news was not well received, and Walter told him that was out of the question. "You are too young; you have no means to make a living and support a family, etc.," Walter told him, but Ralph insisted that he loved his girl.

Wedding in St. Neots; life in California and back to England

Things progressed rather quickly, and Ray, Walter, and I flew to England to attend the wedding of our oldest son in St. Neots on June 25, 1983. Carol and Ralph came to the airport. Carol had a bouquet of Sweet Williams for me. She made a good impression on us. We went to her family for dinner. The parents and a brother and younger sister greeted us. It all went very well, and we were relieved. Carol came from a decent family.

They did have a lovely wedding in an ancient monastery followed by a reception for family and friends. It was a special day. While I am writing this, the two have entered their twenty-sixth year of marriage. They have three handsome boys, who are also my pride and joy.

The two did not have it easy. When Ralph completed his time in the air force they came to the San Francisco Bay area to start their new life. Carol found work in an office, and Ralph started a job for a private airline in Oakland. They found an apartment. Carol's mother came to visit. Ralph lost his job, and a baby was on the way. Christopher was born on October 7, 1984, in Santa Clara. He was a welcome addition to the family. His grandmother came from England for the christening. The baptism took place at St. Joseph's Catholic Church, and the reception at the Le Baron Hotel in San Jose. We were under the impression that things were going quite well, but Carol and Ralph informed us one day they were going back to England to live. That came as a great shock to us. Everyone came to America. Why did they want to go back to England?

On November 14, 1984, we helped them get on the plane. Christopher was not yet six weeks old. We had looked forward to Thanksgiving. I had made arrangements to have the holiday off so we could celebrate Thanksgiving together with the whole family. It was not to be, and life went on just the same.

We hoped for the best. Ralph and Carol stuck it out. They never asked for a dime. We visited them almost every year and saw how well they managed. They had their own way of doing things, but that was OK with us. Had we not done the same?

Over the years they have moved a few times, but each time they bought (not rented) a house. Ralph had then and still does now have a good position at the Birmingham Airport, where he helps to keep the planes in the air.

Ralph chose the right wife, and the two of them together raised a great family. Walter and I flew to England when Richard and Gerard were baptized. Each time it was a special celebration.

The two oldest have completed their four years at the university. Both have good jobs. Only Gerard is left at home. He too will attend a university in the fall. Carol worked at the local school district. When her sons were grown, Carol went back to school to get a degree in accounting and works in a better position for another school.

Ralph and Carol can be proud of their accomplishments. The credit is theirs; they did it all on their own.

A heartfelt congratulations to both of you from Mom.

Ray: high school years, air force, San Jose State, marriage

Ray went to the local high school and made a few good friends. Even though he was handsome, and I believe smart, he had very little self-esteem. Did he, as well as Ralph, get that from me? I too believed that I was not very capable, and that I was not entitled to do the things most girls at my age took for granted. What helped me was working as a waitress in good and well-known hotels and restaurants. I believe that my accent helped me land the jobs to begin with. It meant I had something special going for me. I had a chance to observe how the so-called rich and famous people behaved. They were not different from us.

I learned much. At one time, a well known newscaster told me that I must have had a very good "Kinderstube" (upbringing). It made me feel good. Slowly I dared to come out of my shell, but it had not rubbed off on my boys.

Ray was a dreamer and also very sensitive, not only toward himself, but also toward the feelings of others. One time, about the age of eight, he came home crying hysterically. When I said, "Show me where it hurts," he answered, sobbing, "I can't show you; it is my feelings." This might all be part of growing up, but as a mother you want to ease their pain, because their pain is our pain as well. I am thankful for our Stripe; our dog was licking their faces and made things good.

For a time Raymond did not speak in full sentences. It worried me, and I went to school. The teacher told me not to worry. They would concentrate on that the following year. I waited; nothing happened. Time went by. Ray was about to graduate from high school. The graduation pictures were taken; I had volunteered to be one of the chaperones on prom night when I received a call from the teacher. He informed me that Ray might not graduate because his English was not good enough.

I could not believe it. I decided I would work with him, and we together would succeed. I asked for the material and began to work with him. It was tough, but in the end we did succeed. Ray brought home papers with pictures of little cannons printed on them with the word "dynamite" written across them. It meant he was catching up rapidly. Talk about relief.

During his high school years he worked at Safeway, a grocery chain, first as a bagger and then as a cashier. The last couple of years he worked at the Bank of America. Whenever I went to any of the places he worked, which was seldom, the manager told me how pleased they were with him. He, as well as Ralph, would succeed after all.

In 1983 Ray graduated from high school.

Ray attended junior college for one year before joining the air force. He realized he could do well and gained more confidence. The one year in college already placed him ahead of the high school graduates. He made some friends. We visited him in Seattle and saw that he had adjusted. Ray did not go oversees like his brother.

He was not fond of military life and realized he had to go to college if he wanted to carve out a good living for himself. The air force succeeded in convincing him to go back to school, where Dad and I had tried and had failed.

When he came home, he did go to San Jose State and graduated in international business, with a minor in European history. We were very proud. We felt somewhat out of place at the graduation ceremonies, but we were happy to see our son in the black gown and square hat. He was, after all, the first one in our family to graduate from college.

He started to work at Siemens, switched jobs a couple of times until he landed a job with a start-up company, and worked there for more than twelve years.

While working, Ray moved out of our home and found an apartment in Palo Alto, which he shared with a lovely girl as his roommate. They became friends then, and are still friends now.

Ray too found himself a lovely wife from a good family. Barbara grew up in Colorado and studied microbiology at a university in Durango, Colorado. They met at a dance hosted by the "Tall People's Club." Both of them are very tall, Ray is six foot four and Barbara is six foot one. Ray brought Barbara home one Sunday afternoon. We approved, not that it would have mattered any way, but a little harmony goes a long way. We met Barbara's parents, who came to visit, and again we were very pleased after getting to know them.

Barbara and Ray were married on June 6, 1998. The ceremony took place in a park in San Mateo, near to where they lived. The gazebo was lovely, decorated with fresh flower garlands. A lady minister performed the ceremony. The reception was in the park's recreation center. Again there were lovely flowers on the tables. A sumptuous dinner was served; music was played and people danced. The weather was great. Ray and Barbara had taken dancing lessons and surprised us with their performance of the wedding dance. Dad had made cheesecake as a wedding cake with marzipan roses, etc. Carol and Gerard, my youngest grandson, had come from England for the occasion. The only ones missing were Ralph and Christopher and Richard.

Ray and Barb just celebrated their eleventh wedding anniversary. They have no children; they live in a lovely home on the San Francisco Peninsula in a good neighborhood. Tucker, a big beautiful dog, and Slomo, the cat, are their pets.

Barbara is an independent consultant for pharmaceutical companies.

Barbara, like Carol, is a good daughter-in-law. She likes to cook and entertain, and lucky for me, I do get invited to their home.

They too can be very proud of their accomplishments. I, as a mother, mother-in-law, and grandmother, have no complaints. Considering the distance all of us had to travel to find ourselves and each other, we have come a long way.

Bed and breakfast business

In 1981 Silicon Valley was booming. People moved here from all corners of the world. Hotels and motels were in scarce supply. We had a big house. I felt an urge to rent out our extra bedrooms to the valley companies. Walter took pictures of the house, the rooms and bath. I made a breakfast menu and showed the folder to some of the CEOs who came into the restaurant for lunch. I had waited on them many times and felt comfortable enough to tell them about our intent. They, in turn, were very willing to give this whole idea a try, since they were looking for places to house their out-of-town employees, especially those who stayed for longer periods of time. They sent the secretary over to check out the living quarters, and they were pleased with what they saw. I was in business. The first two guests arrived in February 1981. We charged $25.00 a night, including a generous breakfast of their choice. At times guests would stay for several weeks. We also had repeat business. Some of our guests became our friends, and we are still in touch with them.

One evening a young man arrived from Colorado. He had stayed with us before. He asked if I had cut the boys' hair when they were little. I said, yes. He waited for a moment then said, "Can you cut my hair? I have an important meeting to go to tomorrow and had no time to get my hair cut." So it was; I wrapped a towel around his neck and cut his hair. He was happy.

At times I felt we had the United Nations under one roof. We had this business for six years but decided not to renew our license. New hotels were being built, and our service was not needed as much. It was fun while it lasted.

Flower business

While working in the restaurant, I volunteered to do the flowers for the tables. I love flowers, and it hurt me to see how the flowers were treated. Often, beautiful roses were delivered, all wrapped carefully in wet newspapers. But then they were carelessly placed in a reach-in refrigerator, heads first. By the time we needed them, several heads were broken off. There was not always time to wash the vases thoroughly. The result was that the flowers did not look their best.

Volunteering cost me money. While I was hustling to wash and arrange about sixty bud-vases per week, my fellow workers, men and women, were waiting on guests and made money. I did this for a couple of years; then I offered to do the flowers at home but expected to get paid for it. The company agreed. I did get a license, bought the flowers wholesale, and I was in business.

It was for the money, but more-so for the challenge and for the fun of it. I ended up working in a flower shop later for four years. Walter, my husband, always supported me. There is not an instance that I remember that he let me down. I believe he could say the same about me. We worked well together, whether it was mixing cement or baking cake or bread, which was, of course, his specialty.

A rough awakening: learning about the world and its hypocrisies

The year was 1985. The world was celebrating the fortieth anniversary of the ending of World War II. Here in the United States the celebration consisted of propaganda against the German people in every way and form possible. I felt hurt and betrayed. I remembered my parents and how they had struggled to raise us. My father came out of the war disabled; my mother worked the fields and took care of all of us. Not one of their six children has ever been in jail; not one ever received welfare; not one even was divorced.

Who are these people who dare to slander my parents' character and that of all the other German mothers and fathers who had done a better than average job in raising their children under the most deplorable circumstance? We grew up to become upright and contributing citizen in whatever country the aftermath of the war had placed us.

What was happening? All this after forty years? I could not believe what I was hearing and seeing on television and reading in the newspaper. The United States, which I had always held in the highest esteem, sank to the lowest denominator in my estimation. I began to look at the world differently. The world was not a nice place.

A different yardstick was being used when measuring the crimes of the Germans. It seemed to me that the need to look down on others was so much greater than to look up to someone, regardless of how much we stress the importance of good role models.

Since I have lived in this country, we have looked down on quite a few of our citizens who did not fit the Anglo-American image. The American people seem to be experts at character assassination. We have talked down on the Japanese, the Chinese, the Russians, the Commies, the Arabs, the Muslims, the Iraqis, the atheists, the blacks, the Indians, the gays, the Latinos, and, of course for more than one hundred years, the Germans.

Yet, my observation has been that the American people, like most people, give up their principles rather quickly when the situation calls for it and even commit crimes against their own people, crimes they previously condemned others for. But when the situation changes, even the Americans adapt quickly, for the worse, and expect the world to understand their situation.

America, as a nation of immigrants, can least afford behaving like this. If America expects every immigrant to do his best for this country and become Americanized quickly, we should really refrain from the practice of cutting others down and stop praising ourselves above all others. Eigenlob stinkt (Praising oneself stinks.) is a German proverb.

The older I get, the more German I become. Our upbringing has helped us to deal with the emotional abuse we, as Germans and German Americans, have had to endure for more than six decades.

It does something to the spirit when one is stigmatized as a member of an evil nation. I believe carrying this burden for a long time stifles even the creativity in a person. Can we afford to isolate any group of naturalized American citizens?

The Germans will probably remain in that position as long as there is a Germany and there are people living in that country, who can be forced to pay enormous amounts of money for crimes a previous generation is alleged to have committed. Just recently, the descendents of the Holocaust survivors demanded the German people pay for their visits to the psychiatrist! Wow, to express such a demand takes guts.

I ask you, who is a survivor? I know Jewish people who came to America as early as 1938 who claim to be Holocaust survivors. I cannot see how they suffered as much as did the Germans who were kicked out of their homeland by the millions after the war and chased into the bombed and totally devastated Fatherland. Did they ever get compensation for the land and property confiscated?

Oh yes, we brought all this upon ourselves, they will reason. Everyone was sooo good; only the Germans were sooooo bad.

The trouble is, I could not see it then, and I cannot see it now. American people have never been able to impress me with their special brand of goodness and character. They are people like all peoples. When pushed to the brink, all of them behave in a Darwinian manner; life is for the fittest. The Germans were no different.

Are the victors more virtuous than the Germans? In fifty-plus years I have found no evidence of that. Many thousands of Germans came to America after the Second World War. I still have to meet one immigrant in jail or on welfare. Who are these awful German criminals?

Working in the restaurant business for many years, I was at times reminded of my German background. A busboy asked me, "Is it not embarrassing to be German?" A customer would ask the hostess not to be seated at my table, because he could not stand the accent. Another one said, "You are my servant now; keep that in mind. I am not yours." I could give you more examples, but who am I to feel insulted?

It surprised me that the president of Austria, Dr. Waldheim, who had also been the secretary general of the United Nations, was not allowed to visit the United States. What was his crime? He had done for Austria what every soldier in the world was expected to do for his country. I do not remember reading about Waldheim giving orders to torture the prisoners; nor do I remember that he himself has taken part in torturing others. Again, a double standard is being applied.

Dr. Rudolph, who had worked with Dr. Wernher von Braun on the rocket program in Germany and had been brought to the United States with hundreds of other scientists as war booty, was deported as a war criminal. I could not believe this. If Rudolph was a criminal, he had done a great job rehabilitating himself.

We should have kept him here so he could teach other criminals how to rehabilitate themselves. Maybe the prisons would not overflow. We could have saved ourselves much money.

Rudolph had worked for this country for forty years; every honor the government could bestow upon a civilian he received. America was nice to him when they needed him. Once the mission was accomplished, it was time to discard the old man. How noble and Christian was that?

Rudolph had given all his knowledge, energy, and goodwill to the space program. He and the other rocket scientists succeeded in landing a man on the moon; they, combined, brought tremendous honor to this country. The moon landing is considered the greatest human achievement of all time. Yet, Rudolph's contribution was not enough to allow him to spend the evening of his life in this country with his family. The government found it necessary to buckle under the pressure of the JDL (Jewish Defense League) and discard the old and sick man like an old shoe. He had outlived his usefulness.

Did the American government not use these human beings as if they were machines to further their own agenda? Were they not also treated and used as Untermenschen (subhuman)?

Wow, America acted arrogant and self-righteous, a behavior I despise in people of any background. Have the Germans been guilty of the same behavior? The answer is yes; they too were human, and they too were wrong. This was not the end; more was to come.

I have heard Americans say they would not have needed the Germans to get to the moon; they could have done it themselves. That might be so but when? Was it not of importance to get there before the Russians did?

The Germans could and some did say they did not need the Marshall Plan; they would have been able to rebuild Germany without that help.

Again I say, how much longer it would have taken them to accomplish such an enormous task?

In 1985 President Reagan visited a military cemetery at Bitburg, Germany. Oh, this was just too much. No dead German soldier was deserving of a visit by an American president. These soldiers had been bad, and I know they will be considered bad by the American public for all eternity. After all, all of them were involved in the Holocaust.

Has anyone ever dared to ask, how many "Crystal Nights" the Israelis have inflicted upon the Palestinian people? Do we care and try to stop this terrorism?

The answer is NO. In fact America and Germany indirectly pay for it. Both countries buckle under Israeli pressure. That is how I see it.

Again I ask, what is the Holocaust? Is it a fact that six million Jews were gassed by the Nazis, correction, Germans? (The Allies found all Germans guilty of war crimes; all Germans pay for this in material goods, but mostly they pay emotionally forever and ever.)

How will we ever know what really happened if we are not allowed to examine the Holocaust? History is being revised all the time as new evidence emerges, except when it pertains to the Holocaust; then, we have to accept the truth as others, who have milked the issue for decades, dictate it to the rest of the world. How is it that the number remains six million, when evidence has shown that at Auschwitz alone, instead of four million dead, as was written on plaques from 1945–1989, the count has gone down to as low as 145,000. That would still be too many if you ask me.

What should I believe? If there is such a discrepancy about the count of dead people in one camp, how about the other atrocities? Why can we not investigate? How can I believe anything I am being told about the Holocaust? What are the Jewish people afraid of? Could it possibly break the Holocaust bank along with their special entitlements?

How can I trust the Allies, who very conveniently forget their own war crimes? Was it not a war crime to expel as many as twelve to fifteen million Germans from their homeland in the eastern provinces, where they had lived and worked for centuries? As many as three million of these people died on their way west toward the devastated Fatherland in the middle of winter. And all this happened after the war. I must admit I am impressed by the noble character these Allies displayed. I certainly would not want my children and grandchildren to use them as role models. I see no difference between them and the Nazis, or the Zionists, for that matter.

When I lived in Germany, I never learned to hate the Jews or anyone else, but as an adult observing them, I begin to understand why the Germans could have despised them so much. If they behaved then like many of them behave now, expecting every living soul to cater to their whims and to feed their insatiable appetite for money and their demand for entitlements. Does no one else ever matter?

I do not want to generalize or stereotype and condemn a whole people, like the victorious Allies did to the German people. I try to look at them as I would everyone else, as individuals, and form an opinion accordingly. There are so many decent people among them just like there are decent people among other ethnic groups.

If the Zionists are the chosen children of God, I do not want to have anything to do with that God, a God who loves some of his children more than others. I believe some clever Jews made this story up. One just has to look to Israel and see how their neighbors, the Palestinians, whose land they took and still take, are being treated. To read what is going on in Washington with IPAC, the Jewish Lobby makes me puke. I am disgusted and dismayed.

I grew up as a Catholic and enjoyed all the ceremonies that were part of being a Catholic. I have to say that my parents, and in general the community in which I grew up, took their faith more seriously than most people I have met along the way. They truly shared the little they had with the less fortunate. I have become a nonbeliever, who tries to do unto others as I would want them to do unto me; that is my religion, simply trying to live the Golden Rule. Every religious person prays to his God to be on his side; never mind the others.

As long as we pray God bless America, for example, and at the same time bomb the hell out of others just to keep our luxurious lifestyle intact, it sets a poor example as a practicing Christian.

Who actually believes in the rewards of the afterlife? We all want it now. That has been my observation of all kinds of peoples.

To follow in the footsteps of Christ keeps one on the right track. But what Christian is trying to live that way? Living the Christian life is hard work.

Besides, believing as we have been taught to believe, that Christ is God, makes it impossible for a human being to live up to Christ's standard. I am very comfortable with my spirituality. I try to do my best with whomever I am in contact with and do not worry about the afterlife; I let the chips fall. I wish for my children and grandchildren, and for everyone else, for that matter, to find inner peace as I have found it.

The New York press, 1911; nothing has changed

I came across this speech some time ago. It is as valid now as it was in 1911 when John Swinton, a lifelong newspaperman, said: "Its business (the press) is to distort the truth."

Lester F. Ward, in his book "Pure Sociology" (McMillan, NJ, 1911), said Swinton gave this speech in response to a toast at the banquet of the New York Press Association. I'd like to share it with you.

"There is no such thing in America as an independent press, unless it is in the country towns. You know it and I know it. There is not one of you who dare express an honest opinion. If you express it you know beforehand that it would never appear in print. I am paid $150..00 a week for keeping my honest opinions out of the paper I am connected with.

"Others of you are paid similar salaries for doing similar things. If I should permit honest opinion to be printed in one issue of my paper, like Othello, before twenty-four hours my occupation would be gone. The man who would be foolish as to write honest opinion would be out on the street hunting another job.

"The business of the New York journalist is to distort the truth, to lie outright, to pervert, to vilify, to fawn at the feet of Mammon and to sell this country and race for his daily bread, or, what is about the same thing, his salary.

"You know this and I know it; and what foolery to be toasted an 'Independent Press.'

We are tools and the vassals of the rich men behind the scenes. We are jumping-jacks. They pull the string and we dance. Our times, our talents, our lives, our possibilities, all are the property of other men. We are intellectual prostitutes."

Researching German-American history

Being frustrated about the way the German people were treated in this country by the media, not knowing what to do about this, and to whom to turn, I became interested in learning about the contributions Germans had made to this country in the more than four hundred years of Germans living here. Had this country not been blessed by their presence, I wondered? After all, Germany was the heart of Europe; trade routes had crisscrossed the country from all directions. That exposure must have taught them something, I reasoned. Germany had had an apprenticeship program for centuries; our people had a reputation as being industrious, inventive, and disciplined. Was there nothing that they had done in this country over the centuries that was worth looking at and learning about? Why did our children never learn anything about the German contributions in school? Oh, yes, they had to learn about the Holocaust. How could I forget?

I went to the library and started digging. It did not take long to come up with all kinds of material regarding our heritage, all very favorable. I was overwhelmed with joy. I wanted to share my findings with other Germans, as well as with fellow Americans. I started to make copies of biographical sketches, buildings, newspaper clippings, etc. I asked my husband to help me. He held the old, heavy books onto the Xerox machine while I was writing down the pages we still had to copy. It cost money for the copies as well as for the parking. I insisted I had enough clothes and would rather spend the money for the copies.

I asked my husband to make posters, which he became very proficient at, and enjoyed making them. But how would we display them? We needed a gazebo-type of a tent to hang the posters inside and outside the tent. For years, we loaded all the equipment into and on top of our van and drove to different destinations in the San

Francisco Bay area to show off our rich German American heritage. Once, we even were invited to the Hilton Oktoberfest in Reno, all expenses paid, of course.

We took part in events at least fifteen weekends a year.

At first even our German friends were very skeptical. Neither one of us had ever been schooled in that field. But no educated German people seemed to be interested in their own heritage, and no one else seemed to care. I had waited long enough, and this was America, after all. I just dared and went ahead.

I collected more and more material. Walter, bless his soul, made the best posters. We had flyers to pass out, and after awhile people came to read what we had to offer. We went to school events, high-tech companies, cultural festivals, history parks, and we participated in Earth Day events, Oktoberfests, fund-raising events, events at retirement communities, singing festivals, etc.

We started in 1986 and continued until 2005. It was the year we were going to quit. The Oktoberfest in San Francisco, which always was a four-day event, was supposed to be our last big event. We said so to the promoters and meant it.

Walter passes away unexpectedly

Little did we know that my Walter would die of a heart attack a few days later, on October 21, at 8:00, in 2005. This came as a big shock. Walter had often said, "Schatz, if everything goes downhill from here on, we cannot complain. We have been so lucky." But here he was, dead on the floor in front of me, and I was alive and left behind.

We had forty-five years together, for which I am very grateful. We had at times our differences, but we still had a good life together.

Walter had the biggest funeral I ever attended. The church was packed. People came from as far as Los Angeles, a six-hour drive. The choir sang "Ave Verum," and a soloist sang "Die Uhr" (The Clock), telling about how the heart beats at every trial and tribulation throughout our existence just to stop unexpectedly. His sons paid special tribute to him, and so did a few friends. He would have been proud and pleased. We invited everyone present to The Villages main clubhouse for a reception. Walter was a guy who liked to write things down for the future. We found a piece of paper in the safe on which he had written: "Mom and Dad's funeral, food, wine and beer for all." He said once that he expected about thirty people to attend our funerals, but to his service, 350 people showed up. We gladly followed his wishes. Our sons had made a film of his life. If we can talk about a beautiful funeral, his was one, and I am happy for that.

Our boys were both married; they found themselves good wives from good families. Our grandsons were doing well and were our joy. Two already attended universities. Walter had always been a good provider, and I could continue living at The Villages Golf and Country Club, an active adult community.

Starting a Web site

In 2004, at a neighborhood party, we met a man who created and installed Web sites for nonprofit organizations. I mentioned that I had drawers full of material pertaining to German American history. I wondered if that, too, could be placed on a Web site. He said yes, but no more was said about it. A few days later he called and offered to help me set up a Web site if I purchased the software. His German-born wife must have had something to do with that. I was elated and agreed. So it came about that I now have a Web site. This was five years ago. Last year, in 2008, I had more than 110,000 hits, which means more than 110,000 people looked at some story or article on my Web site. These visitors came from seventy-nine countries. Barbara, my daughter-in-law, suggested a monthly newsletter to keep it interesting.

Now I go through agony every month, thinking of a lead story for my newsletter, but so far I have always been able to think of a subject. I have thousands of pages for my visitors to look at, and they do. This Web site has become my purpose in life. People seem to enjoy it. The computer can drive me up the wall at times, but I keep going back to it and try to solve most problems myself. I predict that I will surpass that number of visitors this year.

Moving to The Villages, a retirement community

In 1992 the homes in Silicon Valley had reached a new height in value, especially in Santa Clara County. Walter and I lived in this big house on a large corner lot in Sunnyvale. We were approaching retirement age. The work was getting to be too much. We thought of selling and moving into something smaller. I had been in The Villages to make a flower delivery a few times and told Walter about this very nice gated community. I was sure we would never live there because this was for the well-to-do people, and not for us.

We went to look at the place and talked to a real estate agent. New homes were being built. We looked at the model homes, and Walter fell in love with one unit, located next to a pond with a fountain in the center and a narrow brook crossed by wooden bridges and a pathway coming down the hill. The view was toward the Evergreen Hills. We decided to buy it with the contingency that we sell our house. Luck was on our side. The first couple interested in our house bought it. Wow. And so it happened that after two months we moved into the new house at The Villages.

It will soon be seventeen years that I have lived at The Villages. Walter still worked four more years at the San Francisco Airport. He commuted every day and never complained. I worked for the visiting nurses, helping mostly old people in whatever needed to be done to make it possible for them to remain in their homes and live independently.

After a few years, both of us were retired. We had a very nice home, in a park like setting, where gardeners did the work. Walter would occupy himself with his hobbies, which were photography, working with the computer, baking, entertaining guests, long walks in The Villages hills, and singing in the German choir, which we both enjoyed. We still attended a few festivals with our exhibit.

As a volunteer in our retirement community, Walter transported equipment such as wheelchairs, bed commodes, walkers, canes, etc. to people who were in need of such aids. The Villages operated a small warehouse to store this type of equipment and loaned it to residents free of charge. He was always willing to lend a helping hand. He was handy and could fix almost anything.

I was a member of The Preservation Action Council, which preserved the architecture in San Jose. They had also been influential in preserving German pioneer houses. Once a year they had a fund-raiser, where they served food and drink and had an auction. Our donation was an authentic German dinner for six at our house, including a tour of The Villages. To our surprise, people paid as much as $2,500 to have dinner at our house. This was no problem for us. Walter and I both had worked in first-class hotels, and it was a challenge to make it a memorable event. Walter would greet the guests, looking the part with his Hamburger Fishing cap and white shirt and dark vest. He showed them our Villages. This was part of the package. We enjoyed doing it.

One of the pioneer houses was moved and incorporated into a new complex downtown to serve as a shelter for homeless young people. The owner of the pioneer house had served the city council of San Jose for six years. Later he served on the County Board of Supervisors.

Adolph Greeninger also had been president of the San Jose Turnverein for many years. The Turnverein was an athletic club, whose motto was "Sound Mind, Sound Body." This group introduced physical education into the public schools in San Jose in 1891. How appropriate to have his home serve as a home for young people.

Since Walter is no longer with me, I am especially grateful to live here. The Villages has much to offer in every field imaginable. It is a gated community and, therefore, very safe. The eighteen-hole golf course is an asset for everyone—for the ones who play on it but also for the residents who enjoy the sweeping views and the different shades of green and water features. Our many miles of walkways and hiking trails are the envy of every Wandersmann. Not a day goes by that we do not see deer, wild turkeys, rabbits, and ducks, and on rare occasions we even see a fox or coyote, or even a bobcat.

Swimming is available throughout the year. We have a well-equipped exercise room, library, and a first-class restaurant. One can take lessons in all kinds of subjects. A resident can attend a lecture or present one, attend a play or be a player in one. Concerts are given at regular intervals throughout the year either by the choir or orchestra or both. We do have a boutique store, and everything sold in it is made by Villagers. People work with wood, clay, paint brush, textile, and other materials.

The needlework takes your breath away. We have a great newspaper, published every week. After having all this for us to take advantage of, I appreciate the great sense of community that prevails here. People visit and help each other. Here, we actually know the neighbors, celebrate together as neighbors, and drive each other to the doctor or beauty shop if needed. Almost everyone who is capable is involved in some kind of volunteer work. We have different ethnic clubs, which are open to every resident.

I feel very fortunate to live here. I too get older, and there is no getting around it. But life is still good. I have a good relationship with my sons and their wives. My grandsons send me e-mails and come to visit on their own, and we have a great time. They don't even ask for money.

My frustration about the harsh treatment by the media toward my people has developed into a passion for German American history, which I share with whom ever wants to take advantage of it on my Web site. It is great to be passionate about something. It keeps the mind active. Not only do I keep busy, but I feel I am still contribute.

Our German club in The Villages is always in need of help. We have at this time 145 members, of which about thirty speak the German language. In 2002 I suggested to use some of the money (some of us cook a German meal for the members and charge for it) to honor a German pioneer who had done some outstanding work for San Jose. We chose Adolph Pfister. He is known as the father of the first free public library. When he was elected mayor in San Jose in 1870 (he was elected twice), he donated his salary and spearheaded a program to establish the public library. He served on the library board for seventeen years.

The members of The Villages German Club donated $5,500 to honor Mr. Pfister with a bronze plaque in the California Room, located in the new Martin Luther King Library which is affiliated with the San Jose University. Both institutions are located downtown. We are very proud of this accomplishment.

In 2006 the Germania Verein in San Jose celebrated its 150th anniversary. To commemorate this event, the members decided to honor one of its earliest members, John Balbach, who manufactured the first steel plow on the West Coast in 1852. He too has a plaque donated by the larger German-American community. It is mounted on the side of an apartment building on Market South Street in the center of San Jose, where his blacksmith shop was once located.

The San Jose Symphony had its roots in the Germania Verein Amateur Orchestra. This orchestra lasted for 123 years; it declared bankruptcy in 2002. The orchestra practiced above the Pfister store as early as 1856, when the Verein was founded. We have a newspaper clipping of a Germania concert going back to 1868.

A large picture of the orchestra was found underneath the Germania Hall in 1987. It shows all the musicians with their instruments and has a name written under each picture. The picture was taken in 1892.

Again, we had a fund-raiser and collected $5,000 to have the picture restored. It found a place of honor in the new City Hall, in the lobby, where it is displayed among other relics from the past.

I am still active in the mixed choir in the Germania Verein. We practice and have two concerts a year in the old Germania Hall, which was built 1893 and was advertised as the first symphony hall west of the Rocky Mountains. This hobby of mine, German American heritage, will never run out of interesting material to discover and to share.

In San Jose, I traced seventy-five pioneers who made a difference for that city.

Have I ever regretted coming to America?

You might ask if I ever regretted coming to America. The answer is no. America has taught me much about the world and about myself. It has broadened my horizon tremendously. I have dared to step out of my comfort zone, to set goals, and try to reach them. It has given me the chance to travel and see the world. American people are tolerant, and when they see you are striving to give your best, they are always there to encourage you. If you fail, you are not being ridiculed but encouraged to try again.

On the other hand, I will say that it was our German upbringing, or one could say the Prussian virtues instilled in us, which were decisive for the success my husband and I were able to experience. I looked them up in the computer after I read about them in a German newspaper. It did confirm what I already knew.

I will list them here: Sincerity, humility, industriousness, obedience (without fear of giving your opinion), straightforwardness, sense of justice (live and let live), religious tolerance, toughness against oneself, courage, sense of order, sense of duty, probity, self-denial, austerity, bravery (learn to endure without complaining), loyalty, incorruptibility, subordination, self-effacement (be more than you seem to be), and reliability.

I am sure my mother did not know that these virtues actually had a name, but she and my father lived them and instilled them in us.

I believe striving to live these Prussian virtues and the Ten Commandments have served us well. Even with very little formal education, we were able to carve out a good living for ourselves and our children. We call America home. I am grateful for everything America has so generously given to us. I do my best to return the favor.

A week in Berchtesgaden

We arrived at the Munich Airport about eleven o'clock Friday morning in August; we picked up our rental car and started toward Berchtesgaden. The weather was beautiful and so was the scenery. We stopped at the Autobahn restaurant for a bite to eat and were surprised by the selection of food. The place was spotlessly clean, and so were the umbrella-sheltered tables outside and the areas around them. The picture-postcard view enhanced the experience. After all, this was good old Germany; we felt at home.

After a couple more hours of driving, we found ourselves in front of the "Ferienhaus Waldheim" (home in the forest), our home for the next ten days. And what a beautiful chalet it was, with geraniums spilling over the flower boxes hanging on carved balconies surrounding the three-story building. The front presented itself with an arched entryway decked out with painted tiles. The side of the house was painted with frescos, and the garage doors were held up by heavy, decorative wrought-iron hinges.

But all this did not compare with the spectacular view we had of the "Watzman" a granite mountain, its peaks covered with snow, reaching into the endless blue sky. Towering pine trees to the left of us, meadows full of wild flowers below, the call of a cuckoo in the distance, a couple of cows grazing, and we could hear the dull sound of the bells strapped around their necks. I felt a lump in my throat and had to swallow a couple of times.

Our apartment in the third story consisted of two good-sized bedrooms, a full kitchen, a sitting room with a corner bench, a bathroom, and a long balcony with table and chairs. All of it was very tastefully furnished in a Bavarian style. The table was covered with a linen tablecloth and a vase with daises and grasses was placed in the center.

In the afternoon my husband, Walter, and I went grocery shopping. We expected our son Ray and his young wife to arrive the next day. It was the first trip to Europe for Barbara, and they had decided to go to the lake country in northern Italy, but the first night they were going to stay with us. We looked forward to having them and hoped for the weather to remain steady.

All went well. Our son found us; my husband could not believe it. He still thinks of his son, now thirty-four years old and six foot four, as his little boy, who needs dad to give him directions.

Yet, we had another surprise coming. Walter had e-mailed his brother about our visit to Berchtesgaden. In the afternoon, while the young couple and I had a nap, Walter went downstairs. He almost suffered a heart attack, for his brother and his wife were sitting on a log in front of the house. They too had decided to spend a week in Berchtesgaden, so all of us could hike together, etc.

This was also a pleasant surprise for our son, who had not seen his uncle for years. We all got somewhat dressed up, and Walter, excited and happy about the circumstances, invited everyone to dinner in a restaurant overlooking the town of Berchtesgaden.

We ate inside, for a thunderstorm interrupted the diners outside. All of us had a great time, including Barbara, for whom we translated. It was great to be alive.

The next morning, and every morning after that, we found a small sack hanging on the doorknob outside the door, embroidered with the words "Our daily bread," containing a variety of fresh rolls. This was such a pleasant surprise. After breakfast, all of us went up the Jenner Mountain, another peak in the Alpine mountain range. We did not hike but took the gondola, two people to a gondola. Again, the weather could not have been better. The trip up took about a half an hour. The views were grand. Dad was taking movies of everything, including Ray and Barbara, who were in the next gondola following us. We saw the hikers on the trails below us; the Enzian (a blue flower) seemed within reach, and in the distance appeared the Koenigssee, (Kings Lake). What a glorious sight.

After getting off the gondola, all of us hiked to the holy cross located at the top of the mountain. There were still snow patches everywhere, creating little waterfalls. We oo'd and aah'd and talked and laughed and finally went down again. We showed Barbara and Ray the village of Berchtesgaden—the churches, the painted houses with their overhanging roofs, the quaint stores, and not to forget the bakeries with their elaborate wrought-iron gelded signs. Our son treated us to a banana split. We went home, wrapped some food for the young couple and send them on their way.

Walter and I sat on the balcony and tried to read but could not keep our eyes off the Watzman. In the evening, we met Werner and Fia for dinner in town. The next day, we were going to hike the Almbach Clam, but Walter had hit his toe on the suitcase. It was black and blue, which took care of the hike for us for that day. Instead, we took a tour to the Eagle's Nest, Hitler's retreat. One could only get there by bus. The road up there was built in thirteen months, we were told, which seemed quite an accomplishment considering the rugged terrain. One must admit, he had good taste, for the view from the mountaintop was again spectacular. The place was very crowded, and we decided to come down after an hour or so. The solid brass elevator, which holds forty-eight people at a time and was built in 1938, took us down in a minute to the platform, where we would catch the bus to bring us into town.

At dinner, Werner and Fia told us all about the hike they had taken and insisted that we too must go to the Almbach Clam.

The next day Walter's toe felt better, and we decided to go on this highly recommended hike. We started out at 9:45 AM. It looked like rain, and we took jackets. We paid our admission at the Kugelmuehle, which was a water-powered mill wheel smoothing boulders the size of four to eight inches and turning them into round, decorative balls.

We started our climb beside the creek, which soon turned into a wild river. The gorge became narrower and so did the trail. The water came down with great force, pounding the rocks on all sides and creating a deafening noise as it was making its way down the mountain. Waterfalls everywhere; rare flowers growing on the edge; pine trees along with beech, oak, maple, and birch standing side by side, some of them their roots exposed, yet, all of them reaching for the sky. Cliffs hanging over the trail made us stoop in passing; narrow bridges crossed the ravine and the white water below us while we were climbing up, holding on to the rope placed along the side. Finally, we came to the spot where Werner had told us to turn right. We had to pass through a small tunnel, and then the hike would become easier, or so we hoped. We left the river behind and now had a chance to chat with some of the hikers we had seen on the way up. Well, we learned that the trail was getting steeper. Steps, at times created naturally by roots or rocks, sometimes cut into the mountainside by men, all of them going up. We were huffing and puffing and realized we were not in as good a shape as we had always believed. Every now and then we rested while other hikers were passing us by; at times it was the other way around, we were passing them while they rested. We were sweating, water running down our back. After about three hours of agony and the experience of natural wonder, we made it to the top.

What did we see? We saw a friendly looking chapel next to a friendly looking restaurant. We entered the restaurant first. Walter had his beer, and I had a tall glass of cold buttermilk. Some of the hikers had already arrived; others came straggling in, but all of them made it.

Walter and I went inside the chapel to say thanks and to admire the artwork and flowers gracing the altar. The chapel was called "Ettenberg." We had another hour to go down to the parking lot.

We were tired, sweaty, but so happy for having had the experience of the Almbach Clam.

At dinnertime, we made spaghetti and a salad. Werner and Fia knew how we felt. We had a good laugh and spent a nice evening together looking at the Watzman and just talking.

The next day was Maria Himmelfarhrt, (Assumption Day), a holiday in Bavaria. The celebration of the mass was to take place outdoors, with a procession through the town to follow.

We made it a point of going to church early to see the village people arrive in their native Bavarian attire. We were not disappointed; people arrived from all directions—young couples with children, old people supported by their cane or a younger person, natives and tourists alike, all of them in their Sunday best. The altar was placed in front of the church in the market square, decorated with all kinds of flowers. Banners were flying from the steeples; the members of the brass band, all in their native costumes, were getting their instruments ready; flag carriers of the different crafts and guilds, some dressed as miners with plumed hats, some as carpenters wearing leather aprons, some as masons carrying their tools with them, all dressed up, were bringing their very old, well preserved flags near the altar.

Six young ladies, wearing exceptionally festive dresses, braids wrapped around their heads, carried a statue of the Virgin Mary on their shoulders. The statue was at least three feet tall; the base was decorated with lilac, peonies, daisies, and other flowers. The choir was getting ready, and at 8:15 AM, mass started with gun salutes from the mountaintop; the choir started to sing, accompanied by the brass band; the church bells rang, and people bowed their heads in prayer. This was the second time I felt a lump in my throat.

After mass, the procession started. There must have been a thousand people taking part, all very orderly and in groups, old and young, nuns and priests, young men and young women, different clubs, etc., and, of course, the priest carrying the blessed sacrament through the streets of Berchtesgaden.

I joined the procession while my husband, standing on scaffoldings, took pictures. We walked for about an hour, singing, praying, and admiring the little altars people had placed in their doorway. Returning to the main altar in the market square in front of the church, we again were greeted by a gun salute, the church bells were ringing, the brass band played, and everyone sang with full voices, "Holy God, We Praise Thy Name." The celebration was over.

We went home to our apartment, paid our bill, received a bottle of wine from the host, said good-bye and drove north to visit relatives. I left with a feeling of gratitude, grateful for the country of my birth, grateful for the culture it has given me, and the strength it still provides. God blessed America, but God also loves Germany. I will do anything to pass this wealth on to my children.

PS: The following year we invited our son, who lives in England with his wife and our three grandsons, to spend ten days with us in Berchtesgaden. Again it was a great time. I believe none of us will ever forget it. It was money well invested, and I am sure it will bring dividends for years to come.

Here I like introduce some traditions and a way of life in the Muensterland

New Year's Eve

As children we were home on New Year's Eve or at least in the neighborhood. The neighbors took turns hosting a party. The children would be in the house next to the party house so the adults could keep an eye on them. Somebody came by every now and then to check on us. We too had a party, with hot dogs, potato salad, sweets, and punch. We played games and could stay up until midnight to hear the big church bells ring in the New Year. Everyone walked outside in the cold to listen and to wish each other ein frohes, neues Jahr (Happy New Year). There was no kissing or hugging. We had a warm feeling inside just the same and had a sense of belonging. Then it was time for us to go home and go to bed. Some of the adults would walk to the market square, where the town's brass band would play patriotic and religious songs.

Karneval, the last hurrah before Lent

Most of the activities take place a few days before Lent. Karneval, Fasching, or Fastnacht, it is all the same but by different names. It is celebrated mostly along the Rhine River, where it was introduced by the Romans.

Residents and visitors look forward to making fools of themselves. The festivities in these regions are as popular as the Oktoberfest is in Munich, but its tradition is much older.

How did all this craziness get started?

People were cubed up for the long winter months in their small, drafty, dark houses. This would make them irritable and uptight. They needed a chance to let off steam. No one was aware of this more than the authorities, who ruled the citizens with an iron fist. To give their subjects a chance to vent their frustration, they gave them permission to rule themselves for the last three days before Lent. The common people chose their prince, created their own court, dressed up in fancy or not so fancy costumes, wore masks, and celebrated their short freedom with gusto.

The roles of leaders and peasants were reversed, and the leaders waited on the common folks. They, in turn, took advantage of this rare opportunity; they ate, drank, danced, and carried on to the point of exhaustion for Tuesday before Ash Wednesday, which is Fastnacht, the night before fasting began.

Has Karneval changed over the years?

The living conditions for most people have improved drastically. Other than that, the "Rhine Laenders" find plenty of reasons to celebrate the old-fashioned way, that is, to the point of exhaustion. Many of the companies in these regions close for a day or two, as do the schools and public offices.

In some cities they have parades. The participants, as well as the bystanders, dress up in fancy or outrageous costumes; the floats often show people with masks, dressed up as representatives in government and church. The object is to make fun of them and embarrass them as much as possible. In the big halls, people sit at long tables, eat and drink, sing, and listen to clowns or jokers, who again ridicule the whole establishment.

The jokers are called "Buettenredner." The name derives from the fact that the joker often stands in a vat (Buett) that was used to wash the dirty laundry. This is their aim, to wash the dirty laundry of the community out in the open for everyone to see, hear, and laugh about.

In between there is plenty of music for dancing and schunkeln (linking arms, moving from side to side with the rhythm of the music).

There are songs written especially for these events. Some of them can be heard for generations, for instance: "Du kannst nicht treu sein," ("You can't be true, dear") or: "Wer soll das bezahlen?" ("Who will pay for all this?"), etc. On Monday before Ash Wednesday, it is the women's turn to let their hair down (Alt Weiber Fastnacht). It gives them a chance to show "who is the boss." They stop any man in the street and cut his off tie.

Even the children get in on the act. They too dress up and take part in the parade or watch it go by. Children often have parties in the neighborhood. They celebrate with soft drinks, potato salad, hot dogs, and Oelgebackenes (doughnuts), make music with old pot lids, washboards, and spoons, and just have a good time.

Palm Sunday is especially for small children

Everyone went to church and often went twice. It was a glorious celebration with lots of music. Also, on Palm Sunday, groups of preschool children carry a palm-stalk through the neighborhood, stopping at every house while singing:

Platt Deutsch: Palm, Palm Poschken, lot den Kuckuck kroschken, lot the Voegelkes singen, lot den Geldbuehl klingen, heisukerey, heisukerey, wen noch enen Sundag is, dann krieg we en eiy, dann krieg we an eiy, dann krieg we an lecker Puskeely.

English: "Palm, Palm Sunday, the Kuckuck is calling, the birdies are singing, the money box is ringing, lalala, lalala, come next Sunday we'll get an egg, we'll get an egg, we'll get a pretty, sweet Easter egg.

The person who opens the door welcomes the children and gives them some change or adds some sweets to the Palmstock.

The Palmstock is made from a freshly cut elderberry stick. The outer rind is peeled off, the stick is scraped all around in about five-inch intervals. Fathers use a dull knife or some other tool; some use a piece of broken windowpane. The thin wooden shavings appear like a ball of curls around the elderberry stick. The shortest stick has two balls of curls for a two-year-old; the largest Palmstock has six curls, which means the child is six years old and will enter school in the fall. Mom decorates the stick. A cake wheel is added to the top of the stick, symbolizing the cycle of life; an orange, decorated with sprigs of boxwood (known as palm in the Muensterland) is placed above the wheel; cookies, candies, a string of raisins, dried prunes, etc., hang around the curls and finish off the traditional Palmstock.

On Palm Sunday, the children can eat all the sweets they want or have, but then abstinence is (or was) the rule until Easter Sunday.

Easter celebration as I remember it

After Palm Sunday, the mood became more serious. Usually the weather was pretty bad. It was blamed on Judas, because Judas betrayed Jesus on Good Friday, or so the Bible says.

The week before Easter was also spring cleaning week. All the drawers were emptied and reorganized. Some of the heavy winter clothes were aired out and put away. The mattresses were aired and cleaned. Even the Schrank (china cabinet) was emptied. The fine china was washed and put back (no dishwasher). The doors in the house were cleaned and polished, and, as I remember it, they needed it. Heating the kitchen and maybe the family room with coal and wood all winter had left a film on everything. Besides, men would smoke a pipe, and on Sunday, maybe a cigar. I do not remember women smoking; it was frowned upon.

The man would prune the trees and shrubbery around the house and in the orchard. The wood was gathered and brought to a designated meadow for the Easter bonfire, which was lit on Easter Sunday in the evening. All this took place even though people worked in the factories or some other place. Somehow, they found time to keep up the traditions. In the evening we would at times go to church for the stations of the cross. On Thursday before Easter, the whole town was involved in keeping watch in the church with Jesus. Neighborhoods were taking turns in attending hours of prayer throughout the night. I enjoyed all that very much. One had a sense of belonging; everyone was pulling in the same direction.

On Good Friday, we ate pancakes with raisins in them. That was the meal for Good Friday, and that was the only time we ate them. Saturday before Easter, I would again go to church and observe the blessing of the wax candles being used on the altar throughout the year and the blessing of the holy water. Then, finally, Easter was here. We all would get up early to go to church to celebrate—"Christ has risen." The organ in the church would roar, and the congregation would sing with full voices: "Das Grab ist leer!" ("The grave is empty.")

We wore kneesocks on Easter, regardless of what the weather was like. Often, we had knitted them ourselves during the long winter evenings.

After church, we hunted for Easter eggs. Our parents had hidden them in the gooseberry bushes or under rhubarb leaves, etc. Sometimes, the pussy willows in the ditch began to show their shiny, furry toes. Of course, I could not resist and picked some.

Noon was the main meal. It was Easter, and we could look forward to a roast, stewed plums, and pears, and, not to be missed, pudding. When everyone was home, all eight of us, we added a small table so we could all sit together. These were good times and left fond memories.

In the afternoon we would be sent to the Christian studies. I always enjoyed the singing. Singing was part of everything. In the evening on Easter Sunday, we could eat all the eggs we wanted. That was really special, because getting an egg on an ordinary day was a rarity. After early supper, we would go to town to join in the procession. People would line up, adults, young men, young women, and the children. We would chant a litany. Slowly, the procession would move out of town toward the meadow, where the fire would be lit. A couple more prayers and the fun could begin. The huge bonfire was lit; we would build a circle around the fire, sing and shout, kick each other playfully, and just have a great time getting all dirty.

The next day was still a holy day. We again went to church, but then it was a day for play. Our parents might visit a relative or check the crops in the fields. The young adults would go to a dance. After all, no dances had taken place during Lent. All were simple pleasures. There was little expense involved but lots of fun.

Springtime is for planting

In my hometown few people lived in apartments and even if they did, they still had a plot of land on the outskirts of town where they grew vegetables and maybe some potatoes und flowers. The soil needed to be fertilized, tilled, raked, etc., before sowing or planting could begin. We learned all that at an early age, not because we wanted to, but because our parents needed us to help, and it was a way of life. Once the seeds had sprouted, and the little plants were a couple of inches tall, they needed to be thinned out. Weeds grew as fast as did the lettuce, spinach, carrots, or beans, etc., and needed to be pulled. On Saturday we would even go to Grandma's house to help there. All the children helped in the fields, and it did not harm us one bit.

May is the month of Mary

It was a custom to have a "May Altar" in honor of Mary the mother of Jesus. The children would go and pick flowers in the meadows and decorate a stature of Mary at the altar. Our altar was a board on the kitchen wall that previously had served as a stand for the radio, (when the Belgian and Dutch soldiers came, they took the radio, among other valuables). In the evening after supper, we would remain seated at the dinner table and Dad would read a couple of verses from the "Prayer Book to Mary." We often sang, since we have many songs in honor of St. Mary as well as songs of spring. On Friday evening we would go to the May service in church. As teenagers we would not only go to pray but also to see if our heartthrob was there also. Just seeing him was enough of a reward.

Labor Day, first of May

The first of May was set aside to honor the workers. There were a couple of speeches in the market square; music was playing, and a flag flew high from the flagpole. As children we were more concerned with our Ausflug (outing). We started early in the morning, walked a couple of miles in the woods, drank our homemade soft drink, ate the sandwiches we had brought, sang "Der Mai Ist Gekommen" ("May Has Arrived"), and then came home again. No one thought of kidnappers, but there was a fear of ammunition and explosives still lying around from the war. This could be dangerous.

The teenagers and young adults would look forward to a dance, and there were several all around town. Alcohol was served to the younger folks as well as to the older. Sometimes you could see a young person stagger, but there was not the binge drinking that I have heard about in the States. Violence was a very rare occurrence.

Pentecost, Pfingsten, Pfingstbraut

It is the feast of the Holy Spirit. I learned at an early age that everything depends on the spirit, awareness, and consciousness. The spirit, or attitude, will either make or break you. I believe that to this day.

As children we looked forward to Pentecost Sunday because it was a special day in all the neighborhoods.

June is the wedding month. The children would imitate a wedding. A couple of children were chosen to be the bride and groom for that day. The kids were dressed up, the boy had a top hat and the girl had a veil (which might have been a curtain taken off the window). The pair was picked up at their house in the pulling cart (bollerwagen) all decorated with birch branches and flowers. All the kids appeared in their Sunday best. We had cake and punch to celebrate. It was much fun.

The second Pentecost Day (Pfingstmontag) was the adults' turn to celebrate. The Schuetzenfest season began usually on the second day of Pentecost.

Schuetzenfest

Summertime for the German-speaking communities meant concerts and picnics in the park, a cool beer in the beer garden or Gartenlaube, or a Schuetzenfest for the whole village or town to take part in. Everyone capable of walking would meet in the meadow and help make the Schuetzenfest a success.

Just a brief explanation of the word Schuetzen, and the Schuetzen Verein's tradition. Schuetzen is a German word for protection. During the Middle Ages, when the cities were protected by walls and gates, it was the responsibility of the various guilds to keep watch at the city gates to protect and guard the citizens within the walls and keep the undesirables out. These guardsmen were called Schuetzen. In later years police protected the citizens, and the position of the Schuetzen became obsolete.

The Schuetzen started a club, met regularly for target-shooting practice, conducted a shooting contest, and combined all this activity with a festival. The best "Schuetze" became king for the duration of the event. He chooses his queen, and together they choose their court. This can be an expensive affair for all people on the court, especially for the king and queen. It is expected of them to spend some of their good fortune on their subjects and troops. This tradition is hundreds of years old and still very popular all over Germany.

I only participated in a couple of Schuetzenfests. During the war these activities did not take place. I left home when I was fourteen years old to work in a hospital in Gelsenkirchen. Later, I worked in households, where it was often my turn to stay home while the others celebrated. I did not mind it too much because I did not know the people in that town. I did hear about the events in my hometown from my sisters or girlfriends.

Farmer's wedding in Westphalia

June is the month for weddings. A "Bauernhochzeit," or a wedding, on a farm was a big event. As a rule the oldest son would inherit the farm. Most families had many children. Dividing the farm among all of them was not a good idea because no child would have inherited enough land to make a living. So, the oldest son paid his brothers and sisters a certain amount of money, and the issue was settled. Often the brothers also were given a chance to learn a trade.

Now back to the wedding. At times, the young farmer tried to marry a girl equal in status or better, who he hoped would bring some wealth into the family. Once a young couple had found each other the negotiations between the parents could begin. How much would the girl bring? Would it be acreage, livestock, a big hope chest, etc.? Does the girl come from a reputable family? Was she efficient in her work? All these were important questions that mattered more than good looks.

When all the details had been worked out to the satisfaction of the parents on both sides, the date was set and the planning for the wedding could begin. Often, additions or changes to the farmhouse were made.

A month before the wedding the "intend to marry" was announced from the pulpit. That was the beginning of the festivities. After mass, the men met in the next "Wirtschaft" (guesthouse) to drink to the young couple's fortune.

Neighbors were engaged to help with the preparation and celebration. They were responsible for inviting the guests, among other things. The relatives of the couple had made several guest lists. The neighbors flipped a coin, and whatever area they had chosen, they went. For transportation they used the bike, which was being decorated for the occasion. The whole affair was not an easy task because the inviter had to recite a poem at every house to which he went. The poem would reveal some information about the couple and the time and place the wedding would take place. For his effort, the inviter would be offered a schnapps.

At the bride's homestead, things were getting hectic. The cow the parents had negotiated over and decided on, was being brushed and cleaned. A wreath was wound for the cow to wear on the way to the young man's farm. I remember seeing a cow with the crown between her horns, passing our house, being led by a young man dressed up for the occasion.

On Sunday before the wedding the young men in the groom's neighborhood would scrub and clean a big hay wagon. The women would make white paper roses to attach to the garlands, made of birch and pine branches, to be wound around the bows attached to the wagon. This was a full day's work, and, of course, food and drink were served, and you could be sure someone played the accordion.

Carts pulled by a horse moved back and forth from the bride's house to the groom's house to bring the hope chest and whatever else the girl would bring to her new home.

Weddings were usually celebrated on Tuesdays. Mondays, the cook showed up. Again, neighbors and relatives helped to clean the vegetables, peel potatoes, and set the tables in the barn, which, of course, had been cleaned. Garlands were attached to the stables; the horses were brushed, etc. On the evening before the wedding, garlands were hung around the entryway of the girl's house as well as at the groom's house. Friends and neighbors would sing a song for the girl, "Mother, give her your blessing, for tomorrow she'll be wed." Everyone sobbed at the end. The next morning, when the girl stepped out the front door, neighbors and friends would stand and wish her well.

She went to church in a coach, wearing a black dress and a white veil with a wreath made of mirth. Arriving at the church shortly before 8:00 AM, groom and bride would enter the church together. The organ would play, and the guests would sing. The ceremony included a mass.

Coming out of the church the big hay wagon, all decorated, was there waiting for them. The coachman was dressed up, and the horses had paper roses in their mane and tail; the church bells would ring; people were standing on both sides of the pathway, wishing them well as the wagon moved away slowly, the wedding party comfortably seated in the hay wagon.

At the groom's house, in the barn that was attached to the living quarters, breakfast was being served, which included buttercream tortes, all kinds of baked goods, Westphalian ham, and all kinds of cold cuts. Always, there was some alcoholic beverage available. Soon the brass band arrived and played, to the delight of the guests.

Lunch, which was the main meal, was being served at the nearest neighbor's house. Again, all was shipshape. Decorations, flowers, and plants were everywhere. The garden paths had been raked and weeds had been pulled. Lunch consisted of beef noodle soup; boiled beef, served separately with an onion sauce; next a variety of salads were served; then came the main course, pork roast, potatoes, gravy, applesauce, stewed prunes, and vegetables For dessert there was pudding and fruit. All the while the band was playing softly.

In the afternoon, the wedding party went back to the groom's house. Now the guests had a chance to see what the bride had brought to her new family. Linen closets were inspected; special attention was paid to bring the girl's needlework to the forefront, where it was examined. China and other valuables were admired.

Now the bride had to prove that she was capable of handling her new position. One of her tasks was baking pancakes over an a wood burning stove. Another task was slicing pumpernickel, the heavy, black bread which is a staple in Westphalia.

A loaf of pumpernickel measured about 12 x 12 x 18 inches. It was heavy. I remember strapping it on the back seat of the bike bringing it home from the bakery. Cutting a thin, even slice needed practice. Yet, if the bride gave it a good try; everyone was happy.

I remember my mother holding the huge loaf on her lap and maneuvering the big knife around the top of the loaf carefully, applying just enough pressure to produce a thin, even slice of pumpernickel.

By then, it was about supper time. Trays of open-faced sandwiches were offered along with potato salad. Again, there were all kinds of cakes available for everyone. The music started to play for dancing. The young couple had the first dance; then both sets of parents joined in, and after a few rounds changed partners. Then everyone joined in. They danced like there was no tomorrow, old and young. It was, and I believe still is, a tradition that the sons dance at least one dance with their mother. I remember going to bed a couple of times hearing the music of a wedding celebration in the distance.

One more note, the helpers, waiters, dishwashers, etc., were usually cousins, friends, and fellow workers. They came to work, but after dinner they were included in the party. They could help themselves to whatever food and drink was available, and there was plenty of both. Besides, who knows, there might be a partner in the wings somewhere to be discovered.

A new baby in the family

Just a few days after the mother came home with the new baby, the neighbors brought her a Plass, which is a huge raisin and fruit loaf of white bread. The Plass measures about thirty inches long, fifteen inches wide and four inches high. The top of the loaf is usually decorated with a fancy braid of dough.

The neighbors dressed up in their traditional clothes of the area, placed the Plass into a pillowcase, and tied it shut on the top. They then placed it on a short ladder and carried the bread to the home of the young family.

The idea behind this tradition is to make certain that the young mother has something in the house to offer visitors, who will surely show up soon to see the baby.

The ladder serves symbolically to give the baby a good start in life, assuring that he will climb to the top. Of course, the neighbors get to taste a slice of the bread with butter and jam, and lots of coffee; maybe even a schnapps.

Kaffeeklatsch

In Germany, and wherever Germans have settled, women look forward to the Kaffeeklatsch. This means ladies meet at a designated house, on a designated day, at a designated time, to have a Kaffeeklatsch, for which one of the lady members of that particular Kaffeeklatsch circle is responsible for that day. They drink lots of coffee and eat cake with whipping cream, talk up a storm, read poetry, gossip, sing, play bingo, or whatever else they decide to do for their entertainment on that afternoon. The table is set with fine china and silver and fresh flowers. Usually the lady of the house bakes her cakes from scratch. They might even have a little liquor as the day progresses.

This is a fun time and feeds not only the body but also the soul.

Wo man singt da lass dich nieder, boese Menschen kennen keine Lieder

Where people sing, it's safe to settle

Last week, April 2009, I received an envelope from my sister that had a self-made songbook in it. She had told me about it on the phone, how much she enjoyed it, and how much fun the seniors in my hometown had had singing the twenty-seven songs. The melodies were all well known, the lyrics were newly made up, all pertaining to the hometown, the event, their age group, etc., (in this case, it was Karnival, (Mardi Gras).

Some of the songs were in Platt Deutsch (Low German) and some in High German. I can just see these people, all advanced in age, sitting at long tables, nicely set, a huge piece of cake with whipping cream and coffee in front of them, singing up a storm and tears rolling down their faces from laughing so hard. I bet that afternoon was medicine for these men and women. There is something to be said about a homogeneous society celebrating together.

Singing was, and still is, a big part of their lives. Most of them do not read music, but I am sure they know many songs by heart. The German people (maybe others too), have songs about everything. They sing about the clouds, the sea, weather, birds and fish, plants, the forest, every trade you can imagine, and every emotion one can experience.

This is really a treasure, and for the singers therapy at the highest level, and it is all free.

> "Of all the arts, great music is the art to raise the soul above all earthly storms."
> (L. Lealand)

Assumption of Mary, August 16, apple procession

In my hometown we honored Mary with a procession. In the afternoon people would gather at the parish church. The procession would slowly move to the outskirts of town, where there was, and still is, a beautiful, very old chapel named Maria Brunn, or Mary at the well.

At the chapel there would be huge baskets filled with apples for people to take and eat. We would spread our hanky onto the grass and sit down. The priest would solemnly step into the pulpit, which had been brought outdoors, attached to an ancient oak tree, and literally give his "Sermon on the Mount" while the congregation was munching on the apples. Then, we would walk through the field, back to the parish church, praying for a good crop.

August: harvesting the grain fields

The wheat and rye was ripe in August. What is more beautiful than a wheat field, golden in color, swaying in the wind? Everywhere the farmers were mowing the wheat and rye with heavy machinery. My parents and uncle next door had only a small plot of land on which to grow grain. They took care of the harvest themselves. The men would mow the long stalks by hand, swinging the scythe back and forth, placing the sheaves in neat bundles, all in a row, while the women would bind them and stake them for drying. The women had made themselves separate long sleeves to pull over their arms and short sleeve blouses. This was for protecting their arms from the dry stalks.

After work it was suppertime, consisting of stacks of pancakes with slices of fried bacon and cups of buttermilk.

On the way home we could hear the farmer sharpening his scythe, which made a ding, ding, ding sound; sometimes we could hear an accordion in the background.

I am glad I experienced this antique way of life.

Richtfest, raising the roof

Whenever a house, a barn, or a stable was being built and reached the stage where a roof needed to be raised, there was a Richtfest, literally raising of the roof. The apprentice had to climb to the top and attach a small birch or pine tree to the gable. Of course, there was always schnapps and beer on such occasions. Later in the evening there was also food, music, and dancing.

There was another custom connected to the building of any structure. From the time the basement was dug out for the foundation to the time the house was completed, the masons found a way of getting their schnapps or beer. When someone not related to the builder or the contractor approached the building site, the apprentice was given the order to go to the person and start cleaning his shoes. Everyone knew what that meant. The man or woman had to dig into their purse and pay for a drink for the workers. The saying went like this: The throat of the mason is so dry from the dust of the bricks, it needs to be oiled.

The workers got their alcohol and continued to work. The phrase "Time is money" had not reached them yet.

Harvesting the potatoes

The days can still be hot in the Muensterland in September, but, already, they are getting noticeably shorter. The grain is harvested in August and stored in silos. Now it is time to harvest the potatoes. We would go to grandma's farm or to any farm in the area to help gather the potatoes into baskets. A couple of horses pulled a machine which dug the potatoes out of the ground, five furrows at the time.

We would all be on our knees, all in a row, crawling slowly forward, a basket in front of us to put the potatoes into. Someone else would empty the baskets into a big cart to be hauled away by horses. We poked fun at each other, joking and laughing while working. This was the order of the day. The older kids would call it flirting.

When work was done, someone would make a fire right there in the field, using dried potato vines. We would throw a few potatoes into the fire and bake them. The skin was burned, but the inside of the potato had a very distinct flavor. When I close my eyes I can still taste those potatoes cooked in the fire on the field. At the farm, the lady of the house and her maid were busy making potato pancakes from new potatoes for the whole gang. That was always a big treat and something to look forward to. But first, we had to clean ourselves up, which meant sticking your legs into a bucket of cold water to get most of the dust off. The boys would also hold their head under the flowing water of a manually operated pump. The girls would just wash their faces.

Everyone sat at the same huge table in the huge kitchen. No distinction was made between farmer and farm hand, maid, grandparents, uncles, aunts, or city folks who had come to help. Everyone got his or her stack of potato pancakes, applesauce, pumpernickel, buttermilk, etc. Someone would say a prayer, and then we could dig in.

Kirchweih: consecration of the church

Our town is ancient and dates back to 839. The towns that have a church have a Kirchweih festival, where the consecration of the church is being celebrated. Vreden had two churches on the Kirchplatz, practically next to each other. The crypt of the Stiftskirche goes back to the year 1044. St. Georg Church, the parish church, dates back to 1478. Both churches were totally destroyed by bombs on March 21, 1945, along with 40 percent of our quaint and pretty town. The Stiftskirche was rebuilt and the crypt restored. St. Georg had to be built new from the ground up.

September was the month where everyone in Vreden and surroundings celebrated Vredener Kichweih, known as "Karmess" in Platt. This took place, and I am sure it still does, every first weekend in September of every year.

The big trucks with the merry-go-rounds, carousels, booth, and whatever else was needed for the Karmess rolled in early in the week. On Saturday, all was ready to go. People would come from all around to celebrate Karmes in Vreden. The borders to Holland were kept open, and all the Hollanders came on their bikes. Many would park them at my parents' house, sometimes ten bikes deep. Sunday morning started out with a procession along the mode around town. We would pray and sing in an organized manner. After church we were allowed to fetch one ride on the carousel, go home for the Sunday main meal, and then go back to the Karmess. We received some money from our parents, but then we knew our godfather or our uncles would also come to the Karmess, and they were somewhat more generous. We would even get some toy or a trinket to take home. The Karmess lasted throughout Monday, starting in the morning with an open market where everything imaginable could be bought, including animals.

These are childhood memories. I am sure they do not differ much from other people's memories, but I began to write them down for my children and grandchildren. I hope to entice some of my readers to do the same; simple pleasures they may have been, but, oh, so precious.

Stomping the sauerkraut

As children in the West Muensterland, we used to haul the cabbage in from the field in a pulling cart (handwagen). The outer leaves of the cabbages were removed (to be fed to the rabbits); the cabbage was cut in half and shredded on a big slicer, which was secured over a big tub. The shredded cabbage was then placed into a barrel, one layer at the time; a handful of salt strewn between each layer.

One of the children in the family was designated to be the kraut stomper. His feet were washed and placed in a pair of new wooden shoes. He was then lifted into the vat to begin stomping the kraut, layer by layer, until the juices flowed. The child would go round and round in his wooden shoes to make sure every inch of kraut was stomped.

The rest of us children were supposed to support the dizzy stomper, but we had more fun tickling and teasing him, since he could not escape and come after us. When the barrel was full and the job was done, the cabbage was covered with a wooden lid then topped with a boulder, about twelve inches in diameter to keep the kraut firm in the barrel. The barrel was placed in a cellar for fermentation.

Sauerkraut:

1 jar sauerkraut (1 quart)
3 slices bacon, chopped
1 lg. peeled and diced onion
1 lg. peeled and diced apple
½ tsp. caraway seeds (optional)
1 bay leaf
4 peppercorns
little sugar, according to taste

Preparation

Press juice out of kraut; place in pot with one inch of water; fry bacon; discard fat; add chopped onion, fry until soft; add this and all other ingredients to kraut; bring to a boil and simmer for about 3/4 hour. Add a little water if needed.

Oktoberfest in Bavaria

In October in the Muensterland, we do not celebrate Oktoberfest like they do in Bavaria. Yet, since Oktoberfest has become very popular in the United States, I'd like to include it and give an explanation of what it is people are celebrating.

The first Oktoberfest was celebrated on October 12, 1810, when Crown Prince Ludwig, later to become King Ludwig I, was married to Princess Therese of Saxony. The citizens of Munich were invited to attend the festivities, held on a field in front of the city gates. Horse races in the presence of the royal family marked the close of the event. The decision to repeat the horse races in the subsequent year gave rise to the tradition of the Oktoberfest.

In 1811 an added feature to the horse races was the first Agricultural Show, designed to boost Bavarian agriculture. The horse races, which were the oldest and, at that time, the most popular event of the festival, are no longer held today. But the Agricultural Show is still held every three years during the Oktoberfest.

In the first few decades the choices of amusements was sparse. The first carousel and two swings were set up in 1818. Visitors were able to quench their thirst at small beer stands, which grew rapidly in number. In 1898 the beer stands were replaced by the first beer tents and halls, which were set up by enterprising landlords with the backing of the breweries.

Today, the Oktoberfest is the largest festival in the world, with an international flavor characteristic of the twentieth and twenty-first centuries. Some six million visitors from all around the world converge on the Oktoberfest each year. The celebrations begin in September and continue into October. Some of the festivities include "Grand Entry" of the Landlords of the Breweries, with about one thousand participants; "Folklore International," with dancing and singing of six hundred selected performers in colorful regional costumes; and a "Big Band Open Air" concert of some four hundred musicians.

Opening day of the Oktoberfest is a sight to behold.

All Saints Day and All Souls Day

Zur Besinnung: something to contemplate.

A Thought

Life is not a journey to the grave with the intention
of arriving safely in a pretty and well-preserved body,
but rather a skit in broadside, thoroughly used up,
totally worn out and loudly proclaiming:
Wow,
What a ride!!

Dunkler Falter

Freiher v. Muenchhausen

Wenn zwei Eheleute zum Sternenhimmel starr'n,
oder ein Bruder haelt seiner lieben Schwester das Garn,
oder ein Freund schenkt bedachtsam dem Freunde ein,-
schwebt ein dunkler Falter ueber den zwei'n:

Einer von uns muss hinter dem Sarge gehn,'
da im Strassenwinde die Schleifen when,

einer von und muss streuen mit kalter Hand
Erde hernieder vom bretteren Grabesrand,
einer von uns muss gehn nach Haus allein,-
lieber Gott, lass mich der andere sein.

Translation:
When a couple gazes at the stars,
or a brother helps his sister winding the yarn,
a friend pours a glass of wine,
a dark cloud hangs over it all.
One of us will walk behind the casket of the other,
one of us will strew the cold earth down into the grave,
One of the two has to go home alone,
Dear Lord, let me be the other one.

In the German-speaking lands people visit the graves of their loved ones fairly regularly, but November is known as the month of remembrance. These are the days that remind us of our relatives, friends, and neighbors who went before us and also of our own mortality.

November 1 is All Saints Day; November 2 All Souls Day; the third Sunday is Memorial Day; the last Sunday before Advent is Sunday of the Dead; (Protestant) the Wednesday before is Day of Repentance and Prayer.

The weather in November is usually pretty nasty. It already is cold and often wet. The wind howls and blows the wet and dying leaves into our faces. Mother Nature sets the mood. We are being reminded of the never-ending cycle of life.

People begin to prepare the graves for the winter in October to have them ready for All Saints Day. The gravesites are being cleared of the summer flowers. If the monument needs cleaning, it will be done. The graves are often covered with pine branches; a few hearty flowers, such as pansies or snapdragons, are planted in between. Some people buy an arrangement and place it near the headstone. Many people place a lantern on the grave and light a candle when they visit. This custom is practiced throughout the year.

People who live too far away, or who, for whatever reason cannot take care of the graves themselves, have the job done by the cemetery gardener. He is hired to take care of the graves, and at times is paid years in advance, to make sure the final resting place of a loved one is not being neglected.

Praying for the departed

Growing up in the West Muensterland, where almost everyone grew up Roman Catholic, these holy days still had another meaning. We said indulgences for the loved ones who had passed on. All Saints Day, as well as on All Souls Day, we entered the church and said these prayers: six Our Father, six Hail Mary, six Honor be to the Father, the Son and the Holy Spirit.

These prayers combined make one indulgence, or Ablass. An Ablass, we believed, shortened the time in purgatory for the soul of a designated deceased person, assuming he or she had not yet arrived there on their own.

Since we as kids already knew several people who had died, and who might be in need of help, these indulgences became a real rat race.

We would rush into the church, mumble the prayers as fast as we could, rush out, reenter, and start the whole process all over again. Sometimes we punched and poked each other and giggled while passing.

Schlachttag, or slaughter day

All Souls Day was usually the first designated Schlachttag. This was sort of a half holiday. It is celebrated on the second day of November. The weather can be pretty cold already.

The butcher would arrive about 5:00 AM dressed all in black except for a white apron and rubber boots. His knives and all the other tools he needed were safely secured in a leather pouch hanging off his belt. A huge kettle of boiling water was waiting for the pig to be scalded to remove the bristle, but first the pig needed to be shot then stabbed in the heart. The blood would gush into a bowl while the front leg was being pumped. I think one could call this a bloody mess.

We dreaded this day because the pig, which we had fed for many months, had become our friend. At the same time we looked forward to this day because it meant fresh meat and sausage. Once the pig was all cleaned, the insides taken out and placed in bowls or buckets, including the intestines, the pig was tied to a ladder, lifted, and leaned against the wall outside to cool. It would stay there all day and even freeze. The intestines were cleaned and washed over and over again and turned inside out. The ends were tied to make them ready to be filled with sausage. In the late afternoon, the butcher came back to cut the pig apart on the kitchen table, separating out the good roasts, the lard pieces, the cutlet, the bacon, ham, etc. Many of these pieces ended up in the salt vat. After weeks, these pieces were taken out and hung on the ceiling for drying, along with all the sausages, bacon, etc.

One thing my mother always did, she had two families, not always the same, for whom she wrapped a couple of sausages and a roast. When it was almost dark, about 4:30 PM, we were told whom to take these to. She said, "Ring the doorbell, put it down, and go away. The people don't need to know who gave the package to them." I mentioned this to her in a letter one Christmas. It made her very happy that I remembered her thoughtfulness.

Anyway, the second day was Wursttag, the day the sausage was being made. The meat was cut and the liver, etc., was ground; spices, which we did not use all year, were used to flavor the sausage. We made all different kinds of sausages. Most were being boiled in big kettles. Other sausages were directly hung off the ceiling to air dry. The whole house smelled like Wursttag. Nothing was wasted, not even the water the sausages were boiled in. The neighbors would arrive with their containers to pick up their Wurst water. Usually, a couple of sausages had burst and that made the Wurstwasser almost like a soup. The Wurstwasser was brought to a boil, thickened with buckwheat flour, poured into bowls, cooled, sliced, and fried in butter. This would make a good supper served with stewed apples.

My aunt and our tenant, who had helped all day, received some of that sausage water but also some sausages. The whole affair was greasy and messy but oh so good.

Schlachtfest, or slaugher feast

Schlachtfest literary means slaughter feast. When I was a little girl, about sixty-five years ago, we could not take it for granted to have fresh meat on the dinner table, especially not during the summer months. In fact, it was a rare occasion.

When I came to America, I was surprised that the German clubs had a "Schlachtfest." The cook bought everything from the butcher and did the last-minute preparations before the guests arrived. Pork roast, boiled pork, and blood and liver sausage were served with mashed potatoes and sauerkraut and sold to the hungry guests. Events often were staged as fund-raisers to fill the club's cash register.

These were, and still are, popular events. Germans come from far and near to take advantage of this rare opportunity to get a "Schlacht platte." Guests rarely worry about calories because they dance the afternoon away to German music. Old friendships are being refreshed and new ones are made. It is always a good time.

St. Nick as I remember it

The Christmas season started officially on the first Sunday of Advent, or more precisely the Saturday before. A bunch of neighborhood kids would go into the nearby forest to gather evergreens and other materials needed to make an Advent wreath or some other kind of Advent arrangement. The older boys and girls remembered from previous years where to find the shiny holly with the deep red berries. We would cut some pine branches and pick the most perfect pine-cones right off the trees. A basket covered with an old newspaper would hold the soft, dark green moss on which we would place all those other valuables we had gathered, including sticks and colorful leaves, which were so pretty that it would have been a shame not to take them. Besides, one could never tell how they could come in handy.

I chose to make an Advent arrangement. Moss of different shades was placed on a large service platter; two potatoes cut in halves served as candleholders for the four red candles. The bases of the potatoes were covered with more moss and colorful leaves.

Last year's red ribbon needed ironing. My mother performed this task by simply holding one end of the ribbon in her right hand and the other end in her left hand. Stretching the ribbon, she pressed it against the hot stovepipe, sliding it slowly from left to right and than once more from right to left. The ribbon began to look like new again before my very eyes. She made a bow, and I placed it, along with a pine-cone in the middle of the moss platter. My creation was complete, and I was happy with the result.

On Sunday at twilight we assembled around the kitchen table and sang, "Advent, Advent, ein Lichtlein brennt" (Advent, Advent one candle is lit) and other songs of Advent.

Also, on that first Sunday of Advent, my younger sister and I would get us a jar and a small box. The jar was for the candies we hoped to get from the baker and the grocer when shopping. We would try not to eat them but put them in the jar until the following Sunday. Each time we managed to deny ourselves the pleasure of eating the sweet treat, a piece of woolen yarn would go into the little box. On Christmas Eve these bits of yarn were carefully placed in the manger to make the baby's bed more comfortable. Of course, this resulted in praise as well as an extra candy from the grownups.

December 6 is the feast day of St. Nick. We really looked forward to this day. On December 5, late in the afternoon, all the schoolchildren gathered in the park near the river, bringing their homemade lanterns with them. All of us hoped to get a glimpse at St. Nick and his helper as they came sailing up the river from Holland.

Moving about to keep from freezing, we waited. Finally, the spotlights were turned on, and we could see St. Nick and Knecht Ruprecht, (that was the name of Santa's helper), arriving. The mayor of the city and other dignitaries were on hand to welcome these very distinguished VIPs. Slowly, all of them walked off the boat. St. Nick was dressed like a bishop, wearing a long white robe, a tall triangular-shaped headdress, called a mitre, with broad satin ribbons flowing down his back. He carried a long cane, curved at the top. He sure looked dignified. His helper was dressed in black. Under his arm he carried a golden book and a black book. We hoped of course, that our names were listed in the golden book. The older kids had told us some scary stories about what could happen to boys and girls whose names appeared in the black book.

Slowly, the small group of VIPs came closer. The city band started to play; all the musicians were dressed in their sharp-looking uniforms. The lanterns were lit, including the torches carried by members of the volunteer fire department. The most beautiful white and black horses stood nearby, prancing in anticipation, waiting for their precious cargo.

Finally, the moment had come, and St. Nick would mount the white horse while Knecht Ruprecht climbed onto the black horse. Slowly, the parade started to move toward town. The sidewalks were crowded with people waving and singing. The brass band was playing. The firemen, with their torches, walked beside the horses. The children carried their homemade lanterns, and the teachers, keeping an eye on all that was happening, kept the parade moving toward the schoolhouse, where St. Nick and his VIPs visited every classroom, decorated by the children in honor of St. Nick.

Being kindhearted, St. Nick assured us that all the children were listed in the golden book, but he also reminded us that there was plenty room for improvement. "Try your best," he said. "Say your prayers and obey your parents and teachers."

We were relieved. Ruprecht, Santa's helper, handed out brown bags, which had a few cookies and candies in them, some nuts, and an apple. At the gate, parents or the older sisters and brothers were waiting to take us home.

But that was not all. The party was not over yet. Overnight, St. Nick would pay a visit to every home. At bedtime we placed a dinner plate on the table in front of our seat. We would make sure that we had laid some hay on the windowsill for the horses.

Early in the morning all of the hay was gone; we knew Santa had been there. Again, our plate had cookies, candies, nuts, and an apple on it. In addition, the boys would receive a pair of knitted socks, and the girls would receive a new apron. Oh, St. Nick was such a good man. He had also found our dog's food bowl, which we had given an especially good scrubbing the day before. Our Bubi, (the dachshund's name) received a few cookies too. But there was something else Santa had brought, and that was a "Stutenkerl," which was not a gingerbread man, but a sweet dough man.

We grew up on dark rye bread and pumpernickel, which is black bread. So, a "sweet, white bread man" who had raisins as buttons was a wonderful surprise, not only for us children, but for the adults as well.

Christmas as I remember it

The sixth of December, St. Nick's feast day, had passed and things were back to normal. We walked to school in our wooden shoes, and on a clear, cold morning we could hear our classmates, who had to walk a mile farther, clamor across the frozen fields, taking a shortcut. At other times, the wind would howl, threatening to cut off the treetops and lift the lonely farmhouses off their foundations. It was dark at three thirty in the afternoon. Inside the house, around the potbelly stove, with apples baking on top, it was very gemütlich (cozy). It was the time of year when even the farmers could spend the afternoon playing cards with their neighbors and have a little schnapps.

The women would sit with some kind of needlework in their lap, gossiping, or as they would often do, singing. The children played hide and seek in the stables, which were separated from the rest of the living quarters just by the milk room. The body warmth of the farm animals kept them comfortably warm. At other times, all of us would sit around the huge table in the huge kitchen, playing board games or question and answer games.

It was a quiet time. During Advent no dances were taking place. Going to the movies was frowned upon. The emphasis was on self-discipline. Mom would bake some cookies, or Stollen, but they were for Christmas, not for us that afternoon.

So it was understandable that we children asked several times a day, "How many more days until Christmas?" I believe Mom bought her peace of mind by getting an Advent calendar for us, so we could cross off a day at a time.

Finally, the twenty-fourth of December came closer. It was time to get a Christmas tree. It had to be just right, not too tall and not too wide. The branches had to be far enough apart to be safe for the real Christmas candles. After all, no tree had electric lights at that time. Sometimes the tree left something to be desired. This was the time when dad got into the act. He would solve that problem in no time. He would cut off a branch here and there and fit them into a hole he had drilled into the stem. Then he placed the tree very ceremoniously into the stand. We all had a comment to make—it is not straight, a little more to the left, now it is just right, and so on.

On Christmas Eve the tree found its way into the "gute Stube" (living room), which in most families was rarely used except for very special occasions. Christmas was certainly such an occasion. We used our living room throughout the winter months. The furniture was simple but sufficient. There was a big table, six chairs, one couch, an old-fashioned sewing machine, and a potbellied stove. It was easier and less expensive to heat that room than the big kitchen.

The children went into the forest to gather moss, branches, holly, pebbles, etc. We needed the material for the Krippe (nativity scene), as we would call it. We helped with everything except with the decorating of the tree. Christmas Eve, we all sat in the "gute Stube." We sang Christmas songs, and the children recited poems they had learned in school. Mom would serve some apple juice in a wineglass, so we could toast with the grownups, who drank something a little stronger. We would crack some nuts and have a few cookies. At bedtime, we placed a dinner plate on the table in front of our seat and hoped Christkind, or as they would say in English, the baby Jesus, would visit and bring us a few gifts.

We had been good; the pieces of woolen yarn placed in the manger would prove it. Every time we had denied ourselves some pleasure during the Advent season we had placed a piece of yarn into the manger to make the bed just a little more comfortable for the baby.

Christmas morning, at 5:00 AM, was the Christmesse (Christmas mass). Every man, woman, and child who could possibly come, would attend. People came on foot, by bike, by horse-drawn coach, or, as the very well-to-do farmers did, by car.

The church bells would ring very loudly, and everywhere one could hear the people shouting, "Frohe Weihnachten, frohe Weihnachten" (Merry Christmas). The church was packed, and the singing was grand and powerful. A big pine tree would stand next to the altar. After mass, we were eager to go home, because we still did not know if the Christ child had visited and if we had received a few gifts.

We were pleasantly surprised. Our dinner plates were buried under the gifts. Besides an apron, mittens, and a scarf, I received a box with glass pearls, which I could string up to make a coaster for the coffeepot, or even a necklace. Under all these wonderful presents there were more cookies and even an orange and a chocolate bar.

The tree looked great, all decked out with silver bulbs and tinsels, and, of course, the burning candles. Our little dog, Bubi, had received some cookies too, just as he had when Santa Claus had visited. And last but not least, Mom was happy with the pot holders I had made for her, and Dad liked his white handkerchief.

Then, it was off to the neighbors to see what gifts our playmates had been blessed with.

Oh, Christmastime was the best time of the year. Every evening, including the sixth of January, the day we celebrated the visitation of the Three Wise Men in Bethlehem, we turned off the light switch, gathered together, lit the candles on the tree, and sang all the Christmas songs we could think of, and there were many.

Eventually, the tree started to shed its needles; the bulbs found their way back into the boxes, and they took the magic with them until next year.

Here I'd like to add some letters that I have sent and received over the years. They express my views on issues of our time. It might not be politically correct, but this is what I believe. Some of the letters to the editor have been published. I do want my sons and grandsons to know what I stand for. I do not expect them to agree.

Tribute to the German mothers and grandmothers of World War II

Mother's Day 2005

The world will acknowledge and even celebrate the sixtieth anniversary of the ending of World War II. Allow me to say "thank you" to the German mothers and grandmothers of that era.

Much has been said and written about our people in the twentieth century. For decades their character has been attacked; my people have been ridiculed, and their souls trampled upon with a consistency and viciousness that at times has overwhelmed me.

This has left a profound impression on me and has affected the way I view the world around me. The more I look and compare, the prouder I become of my people, of my heritage, and especially of the mothers and grandmothers who raised us. Our parents, but mostly our mothers, (their husbands doing their duty in battle) did a better than average job raising us, and they did it under the most adverse circumstances.

With a war raging all around them, with bombing raids that would not stop, with hunger as a steady companion, they gave us love and even a sense of security. They taught us valuable lessons in how to endure and survive and still remain humane.

The German women from the Eastern provinces experienced expulsion from their beloved homeland, in which their ancestors had worked the soil or tended shop for centuries. They faced deportation to a ravaged "Fatherland," which they had only heard about as a faraway place. Finally, all the survivors learned what it meant to live with Allied occupation, accusation, and degradation. Through it all, and for many of them for years to come, they harbored the fear that their husbands and sons may never return. This was an additional emotional burden.

Germany was devastated, our fathers either killed or in prison camps, our homes, schools, and churches destroyed, everyone deprived of the bare necessities; yet, our mothers kept the light burning.

They taught us by example how to be superhuman, how not to lose faith and self-respect, how to respect and have compassion for the hordes of hungry, homeless people wandering aimlessly in the country side; they taught us respect for the aged, the ill, the feeble, the handicapped, the crippled and retarded, and last but not least, respect for the dead. It did not matter whether the soldier buried in the ditch behind the house was one of ours or the enemy. We were encouraged to put flowers on his humble grave and say a prayer.

Our mothers taught us respect for God's creation as well as for the works of men.

They taught us how gratifying a job well done could be. They taught us to love music and how to sing, to recite poetry and memorize proverbs so full of wisdom and joy and so soothing to the soul in good but more so in bad times. Our mothers, in their conscious or unconscious minds, must have known that their effort was not in vain; they must have known that they were raising a generation of responsible adults, stronger through the experience of war, self-reliant, trying their best for family, community, and country.

I believe the results are obvious. It is not by chance that Germany, in spite of its difficulty at this time, is still called the "Engine of Europe." The German immigrant, wherever destiny has placed him, is rarely a burden to society but is almost always a contributor. Many, many thousands of displaced German people made America their home after the war. Not many, if any of them, ever landed in jail or collected welfare.

This has been my observation during the fifty-plus years I have lived in different states in this country and also during my travels abroad.

I am indeed proud of my upbringing, but I am also humble and full aware of the responsibility handed to me in the cradle. I try to bloom where I am planted.

Thanks to our mothers, who deserve the credit for a job well done.

Thanks, Mom, and may you rest in peace.

Hans and Trudy's golden anniversary
Kletke

(Their names were changed to protect their identity.)

This is a story that should be entitled "Against all Odds," for these two people, who's fiftieth wedding anniversary we celebrate today, had a beginning most of us only read about in novels.

Hans was born in the center of Germany, in the Harz Mountains in a town called Ascherleben, in 1924. His father worked for the railroad, which was considered a better than average position. Hans lost his mother at an early age and he and his father lived together for several years. After completing his school requirements in the public schools, he went to trade school to learn how to build airplanes. An apprenticeship in that field promised a good and secure future, or so he thought.

Hans was drafted into the German army in 1943 and everything changed.

In 1944 he was captured by the Russians in Romania, taken prisoner and sent to a camp on the shores of the Volga River. Luckily for him, the Russians needed craftsmen like Hans, and he worked in a machine shop, while most of his fellow prisoners worked in the forests cutting down trees. This was not so bad in summer, but the Russian winters were harsh and merciless. Many comrades died from exposure and lack of food. Four years later, in 1948, Hans came home to Ascherleben.

Remember, the war had ended in 1945, but the Russians kept the German prisoners as slave labor.

His father had remarried, and Hans and his stepmother did not get along too well, so Hans left home after two weeks. His hometown now belonged to East Germany, a country that had not existed before, and, worst of all, it was under communist rule. Hans had had a taste of what that was like in Russia, and he was determined to cross over to the West for a chance of a better life.

The first night in freedom he slept in an air raid shelter in Hanover, where he learned that Berlin was cut off from the West and that the Berlin Airlift was in operation. The Allies supplied Berlin with the necessities, and the city survived. The planes also dropped some raisins, and the Berliner children called the planes "raisin bombers." Hans went to the American air force, applied for a job, and started to work the next day in Fassberg, in the Lueneburger Heide. A fellow worker told Hans about a Mandolin club he belonged to, of which Trudy, his future wife, was also a member. The friend invited both Trudy and Hans to his house, and that is where the couple we honor today met. We'll get back to that later.

Trudy was born in Poland into a farm family in 1927. She had a brother three years older and one five years younger. The German people had lived in this part of the world for many, many years, but after the First World War the Allies had granted the region in which Trudy was born to Poland.

In 1939 the German army recaptured what they believed was rightfully theirs. Life was still pretty peaceful. In 1942 a little sister was born, but luck turned on them when, one year later, Trudy's mom died. The father was fighting the war somewhere on the battlefield. Trudy became the sole caretaker of the family. Her oldest brother, Heino, also was drafted.

In 1945, the Polish government gave orders to all Germans living in that area to leave at once and move west, in an ethnic cleansing campaign. The Russian Front was very close now, and "We children were all alone," that is how Trudy described the situation to me some time ago. Trudy, her little brother, and her three-year-old sister packed some of their belongings onto a wagon, harnessed the horses, and off they went, never to return.

It was the winter of 1945, and what a winter it was. They joined other refugees on the refugee track, passing bombed-out cities on their way until they finally came to West Germany, to a town called Holdenstead. It was June now. They were assigned two rooms at a farmer's house. The war was over, but hunger was still a steady companion, and food was still scarce. Trudy did not know that her father was alive and in a Polish prison camp. He died there one year later. Heino, the oldest brother, found them in Holdenstead and joined them. Time passed and things began to look up. Trudy joined a mandolin club, and being pretty, good-natured, a good singer, and a mandolin player, she, of course, was popular and was asked out on dates. These young men were very surprised when Trudy showed up with her little sister, but Trudy brought her along anyway. Music and singing worked like medicine for Trudy. That was true then as it is now. One day at rehearsal, she met this skinny young man whose name was Hans.

Was it a case of: misery looking for company, two lonely people together, or love at first sight? I don't know.

They got married in November 1950. They were very happy, even though the two-room apartment now was home for six people. Things began to get better. Brother Hermann graduated from school and found work on a farm. At least he would be fed. Heino got married in 1950, and he too moved out. That gave them one more room. After a while Helmut was born, and Trudy and Hans were very happy, but Hans had difficulty finding a job in his field in this little farm town.

They picked berries in the forest and sold them, gathered wood to heat the apartment, and stole potatoes and vegetables from the fields to feed the family.

Four years later Peter was born; prosperity had still passed them by, but they were grateful for one thing, they all were together.

Hans decided to try his luck in Stuttgart with the American forces. It was a faraway place. In order to have money to pay for the train fare, Hans sold his bike. He got a job and sent money home on a regular basis for all of them to live better, but he himself could only come home twice a year. On one such visit, the boys did not recognize their father. This made Hans very sad. He looked for a job closer to home and found one in Bielefeld at Ruhrstahl, and he came home every other weekend. But they still lived in the same two-room apartment. Still, no apartments were available.

Then Trudy and Hans decided to emigrate to the United States of America. They arrived in October 1956. The Lutheran Church was their sponsor. They came directly to San Jose, California. Hans found work at the Ford Motor Company. They rented a house. One year later they were able to make a down payment on their own house. Hans and Trudy joined the German club, where they met people with similar stories to tell, and where they made lifelong friendships. Trudy joined the choir and remained a faithful member for thirty years. Singing helped her to conquer most hurdles life placed in her way.

In 1962 Trudy's little sister married a German man. The two brothers, Hermann and Heino, immigrated to Wisconsin. Heino moved back to Germany after living in the States for twelve years. Both brothers have passed on.

Hans and Trudy went to Germany for a visit in 1992, where Trudy met her in-laws for the first time. When they came back they sold their house and bought a lovely home in Modesto, with pool and all. Their children are grown; the family is intact, and that includes the children of the brothers, with whom they have a close relationship. The only problem is, Trudy is sorely missed in the choir in San Jose. Conclusion and lesson: life is good and worth living.

Second thought: it must have been love at first sight after all.

Congratulations,
Hoch solln sie leben, hoch solln sie leben, dreimal hoch.

We must know our homeland in order to love it

I think it is important to know the geography, the history and the people of the country we call home. We should also try to learn about our own ethnic group to enrich our lives by connecting to the people of the past to build a chain of continuity. It gives us a sense of direction for the future.

I am not talking about our ancestors in Germany but the pioneers with whom we share a common background, who came here many years ago and helped build this country into the envy of the rest of the world.

America is a nation of immigrants. Each ethnic group has contributed to the prosperity of this country and is proud of having been part of this endeavor. It is no different for the German-speaking peoples, who came to Jamestown, Virginia, as early as 1608. The stream of German immigrants has at times slowed down to a trickle, but it never fully stopped. Being an immigrant myself, I wondered if this country had been blessed by our arrivals. I had to find out.

The public libraries were a good start. These institutions proved to be a treasure chest, full of information about my people and their contributions to this country over the past four hundred years. The Germans practiced the trades they had learned in the old country and contributed as architects, builders, railroad engineers, map makers, explorers, manufacturers, merchants, entrepreneurs, farmers, blacksmiths, artists, craftsmen, teachers, ministers, potters, scientists, captains, musicians, soldiers, etc. Getting to know our German American heritage brings us closer to our roots in this country, our chosen Heimat (Homeland).

My husband and I wanted to share our findings with fellow Americans to encourage them to learn about their own heritage and be proud. We took our wandering exhibit all over the bay area for all kinds of occasions. In 2004, we became high tech and started a Web site, which in 2008 had more than 110,000 visitors. We provide information to the German Americans and to the general public to learn about our heritage, which is their heritage as well.

I lost my partner of forty-five years on the twenty-first of October 2005. He suffered a massive heart attack. He did live to see our work being appreciated, for we received the "Friendship Award" from the German government in the year 2000 and the "Distinguished German American Award" for the year 2003.

Purpose of Exhibit

A man once asked me:" Why are you doing this? Why go through all the trouble to have an exhibit?"

I gave this question some thought and wrote my answer on this flyer to explain to myself and others the purpose of our exhibit.

By showing and sharing in the contributions of our people, we share in their struggles and in their triumphs.

Every immigrant experiences the pain of being uprooted and transplanted, the feeling of being lost, misunderstood, out of place, and at times out of control; the agony of learning a new language and losing the children to a culture the immigrant can never fully embrace.

The immigrant finds strength in his roots. His culture has served him well; it sustains him and strokes his soul when the chips are down, and it is all he knows. He is determined to pass the strength and the comfort it provides on to his children. They deal with their own pain, not knowing the old ways and wanting desperately to be part of the new environment.

The children wonder how they can overcome this hurdle without hurting the parents too deeply. These feelings and experiences are universal, regardless of which continent the immigrant came from.

By becoming aware of the contributions and accomplishments of these pioneers we are sharing in their immigrant experience. They too had to overcome adversity and prejudice; yet, they rose above it.

Let them serve as an inspiration to all of us regardless of our background. Together we can make this country a better place.

The German Hausfrau, an endangered species?

(I believe their motto must have been: Spend less, live better!)

I am convinced that the German Hausfrau, as my generation still knows her (I am seventy plus) is on her way out. This, I think, is a tragedy and should be prevented at all cost. What the world needs more than anything else is "German-style housekeeping schools," where young people learn how to manage a household and make a comfortable and cozy home.

If an executive would manage his company the way most households are being run, the company would be out of business within a year.

How do I dare make such a statement?

My husband and I managed apartment houses for more than fifteen years. For thirty years I have worked in the restaurant business, which is closely related to housekeeping. Before my retirement, I decided to do my duty to the community by working as a homemaker for the Visiting Nurses Association. I worked in that position for 3½ years. In our German Club, I represented the Sunshine committee for almost seven years. It was my duty to visit our members who were advanced in age on their birthdays and also when they were confined to bed for longer periods of time. I made an average of sixty visits a year.

All these positions, menial as they may seem, gave me plenty of opportunity to observe and study the living habits of many different ethnic groups and nationalities. Without hesitation I proclaim the German Hausfrau superior to all others.

Of course, I admit, there are exceptions.

I have always enjoyed visiting with people who were quite a bit older than I was. I learned through casual conversation with my German ladies that almost all of them had taken some housekeeping courses when they were young. They had learned how to cook, bake, sew, do the laundry (wash the delicate pieces by hand), tend the garden, and preserve the fruits and vegetables the garden produced. These ladies had done an exceptional job and were happy and proud to talk about it. The housekeeping, they said, had been a minor part of their activity. Child rearing and being a partner to their husbands had taken priority. That might have been so, but the cake they served when I visited was still made from scratch; the coffee table was set nicely with a pretty tablecloth, real china, and a few flowers from the garden in a sparkling crystal vase. The houses or apartments were well taken care of, and if there was still a partner I could be sure that the preparations for the dinner had been started. These ladies were also well educated by our standard. They could recite poems several verses long, they knew many songs by heart, and some of them had been choir members for as long as their voices permitted them to sing. They knew proverbs for every occasion and situation full of joy and wisdom.

My own mother-in-law, ninety-four years young, knew more about nutrition than I will ever be able to remember.

Driving home from these visits, I often felt enriched and recalled my own youth. I felt very fortunate to have grown up in a household where home smelled like home. At times the fragrance of fresh bread from the oven was sooo inviting; other times the soup simmering on the back burner made the wait for dinner seem much too long. On Fridays, the no-meat day, Mom made pancakes, either apple, blueberry, or potato pancakes, with homemade applesauce.

Saturday was a different story. Dinner was a one-pot boiled meal—vegetable potatoes, onion, and some sausage or other meat—all boiled together in one pot; salt and some nutmeg to taste made it a delicious meal. Sometimes, the cooking was done early in the morning. To keep the dinner warm, the contents of the pot was ladled into a bowl and covered; then the bowl was carefully placed in bed between the covers to keep warm until dinner.

Saturday was cleaning day, and the house smelled like soap and Ajax, or Ata, as we would call it. The house was being cleaned, the windows washed, the floors scrubbed, and the garden-path raked. Then, of course, it was time for all of us to get cleaned up, one after the other. Keeping enough hot water on hand was a chore in itself.

Sunday, of course, was church-going day, but Sunday was also the day we had pudding with raspberry syrup for dessert. This appeared to be universal, for every kitchen windowsill had a bowl of steaming pudding sitting on it to cool. With no refrigeration, the Hausfrau found ways to improvise.

The German Hausfrau is aware of the fact that "Love finds its way through the stomach." Another proverb says:"A woman can carry more money out of the house in her apron pockets than a man can haul in with a cart."

I have concluded a long time ago that the old fashioned German Hausfrau is very much aware of her position in life. She uses her mind to invent, her hands to create and distribute, and her heart to enjoy. She is a master improviser if the situation calls for it; and last but not least, she is hard on herself and would easily pass an arduous endurance test. She does not waste time chasing rainbows; rather, she blooms were she is planted. She certainly can be proud of her achievements and her enormous contributions to society. No money value can be placed on the benefits we have received. We are very grateful indeed for having had the opportunity to grow up under the wings of a German mother and Hausfrau.

Maenner moegen wohl die Zeiten bauen; es lebt oder stirbt ein Volk an seinen Frauen.

Men might make history, but the well being of a people is in the hands of its women!

MB.

Letter to Richard, my second grandson

(This is a reply to the letter he wrote to me
at the passing of his grandfather.)

Thursday, November 24, 2005

Rich, I am using the computer. I need the spell check.

Dear Richard:

Today, we celebrate "Thanksgiving" in the United States. I too have much to be thankful for. First, I would like to thank you for the beautiful, long, handwritten letter I received from you the other day. You made me happy and proud. I am glad you are working so hard. It will all pay off in the future.

Yes, I was very happy to have Ralph and Caroline here with me and Ray and Barbara. They were a great comfort and help. Opa would have been very pleased to see the way they conducted themselves and praised him publicly. Opa did not suffer, not even thirty seconds. That is something to be grateful for. We had forty-five years together; we struggled with the language, new way of life in a foreign country, but we had each other, and that was enough to sustain us. We respected each other, and I can say our love grew as we got older. For all this I am thankful on this Thanksgiving Day.

Rich, you are a good writer. I like to read what you have written about the Grimm brothers. I know, they collected many old stories and fairy-tales delivered by word of mouth from one generation to another. These old stories tell much about the evolution and mindset of a people during the different epochs.

Keep an open mind, don't believe everything you hear; give people the benefit of a doubt, and treat everyone like you would want to be treated.

Opa set a good example. He would have never believed he touched so many people in a positive way. People traveled for hours to pay their last respect. He was a simple guy, with little education, grew up during the Hitler era; yet, he made a difference. We received about three hundred cards, and one quality people pointed out most was, you could always count on Walter. He was a man of his word, and it did not matter who the person was he was trying to help; he just did it.

He loved his music. Neither one of us can read music, but we loved to sing and listen to good music. I am happy for you to be able to go to these concerts. I might do some of that myself in the future. We have a nice orchestra here in The Villages, and sometimes they have a guest orchestra or performers to enhance their program. Brahms wrote the famous lullaby, "Guten Abend, Gute Nacht." We often sing that song before we go home after a party or get-together.

I look forward to Ralph's and Gerard's visit. I think we will have a good time and so will you on New Year's Day, when they come to visit you. Enjoy; life is great. Make the best of it, and follow your own inner voice.

All the best, and thanks again.

Oma

Pacific Singing Society visits Philadelphia

(Credit is given to people who demand it,
not necessarily to people who deserve it.)

Working with the public for many years I had a chance to observe and study human nature and behavior. This has become my favorite sport. Contrary to what my German mother taught me, I learned a long time ago that the English proverb "Nice guys finish last" is very close to the truth.

Recently I turned the clock back to the time when I entered this country some forty-four years ago. The urge to reflect was prompted a couple of weeks ago when forty-seven singers flew from San Francisco to Philadelphia to attend the 150th anniversary of the Northeast Singing Society of North America. This event presented German culture at its finest.

I believe, everyone who attended would agree that the whole affair was an uplifting, inspiring, and rewarding experience. We joined 450 singers, who belonged to the above mentioned umbrella organization and had sung together for many years; but this was special, and a special effort had been made to attend choir practice regularly. The old songs had not lost any of their power and sweetness. Our souls were caressed as the sounds of the orchestra and voices filled the big hall. This was more than entertainment; this was a happening, indeed and it was a German

American happening. I looked around. Where was the press? Where were the television cameras?

Did the media not know about this or did they not care? I wondered. One never gets quite used to being ignored, especially when something so beautiful takes place; one would want to share it with the whole world.

Well, there were a few more glitches, as they say in the computer industry, meaning a few things went wrong, and I could not help but wonder if they would have gone as wrong had we been members of a different ethnic group.

When our bus arrived at the hotel a few days prior to the festival, no one knew we were coming, even though the rooms had been paid for in advance. I felt somewhat disappointed. After all, this was Philadelphia, the birthplace of our adopted Heimat (homeland), where more than three hundred years ago our ancestors had landed and founded German Town. Weren't we members of the largest ethnic group in America? This was not a second-rate hotel, mind you.

After about a half hour of wondering what to do with us, the manager finally found the reservation contract in the computer. No big deal, we said, these things do happen; don't take yourself too serious, I thought.

The following day the singers from the surrounding areas arrived, and to quite a number of them the same thing happened. The fact that 450 singers, not counting the people who came to listen to the concerts, had chosen this hotel to have all their activity connected with the festival, including dancing, dinners, and breakfasts, did not seem to matter.

Again I wondered, did we belong to the wrong ethnic group? This negligence could not possibly be a daily occurrence. How could the hotel stay in business?

The next day, a day trip was scheduled for our group. The bus arrived on time, but the bus driver did not know where he was going. After using the cell phone of one of the passengers on board to confer with the bus company, we arrived 1½ hours late at our first destination. This, of course, delayed and shortened all other visits to the points of interest we were to see. No apology was given. Since we had come from all across the country to Philadelphia, repeat business with our group was very unlikely. The money had been paid. We were convinced the driver practiced at our expense. But who cares; no reason to get exited, these things do happen.

In the evening, the first concert took place preceded by a buffet dinner and followed by a dance. A six-piece band played for our dancing pleasure. Of course, dancing makes one thirsty, and a glass of wine or beer gives welcome relief. When we returned from the dance floor, to our surprise we found the table cleared. Some of the glasses had still been half full. The wine was not cheap, yet it was gone. The bar closed at 11:00 PM, we were told, even though the music continued to play until midnight. I could not help but wonder, is it us? Why are we being treated this way? Is this normal? Is the guest not king anymore? Am I getting old? Am I overly sensitive? Have I lost touch with mainstream America?

Sunday was supposed to have been one of the highlights of our trip. We were scheduled to sing during high mass in the cathedral. When we arrived, all 450 singers, we were told that a mistake had occurred. The high mass was scheduled to start an hour later, and the church choir would sing. We were asked to sing in the parish chapel, adjacent to the cathedral, instead. We filled all the pews. There was hardly room for the parishioners.

The monsignor, who celebrated the mass, was noticeably irritated. While we were singing, he interrupted by saying his prayers aloud, facing the congregation and motioning with his hands to stop singing. His sermon was about brotherly love, but he obviously did not practice what he preached. Twice, a collection was held. No explanation was given why there were two collections. As a Catholic, I was embarrassed for the non-Catholic singers by the behavior of the monsignor. I left the church with a discomforting feeling in my stomach. What had happened to my heritage? Is it any wonder that our young people will not flock to us when we allow ourselves to be treated that way? One would assume that the 150th anniversary of a singing society in the United States would deserve some recognition, after all. One hundred fifty years ago the United States was still scrambling for its own identity. This is a country redefining itself over and over again. To have anything last for 150 years is unusual and, I believe, proved to be worthwhile and beneficial to the community.

To be ignored by the Catholic Church as these singers were is nothing short of blasphemy, especially when one considers that most sacred music is German music. Here we were, 450 singers looking forward to lifting our voices and singing to the glory of God and to the delight of the congregation; to be told that plans had changed was very disappointing.

I ask myself, has the twentieth century been so harsh on us that we have forgotten what it is like to be treated with respect? I believe the German people, populating the heart of Europe and being the largest ethnic group in the United States, have contributed more than their share to Western civilization. If any people in this country are deserving of respect, it is the German people; yet, as a people, we are being kicked from all sides. We should have learned a long time ago that the respect we deserve will never be given freely; we must demand it just like all the other ethnic groups demand it. We must not give in to empty excuses. Let's start today.

I do not want to close without giving credit where credit is due. The host choir in Philadelphia deserves all the respect and applause we can shower on them. The work involved in staging a festival such as the 150th anniversary of the North-Oestlicher-Saengerbund can only be appreciated by people who are themselves involved in such activity. In spite of the few mishaps mentioned above, we returned home lighthearted and inspired, thanks to all the friendly people we were fortunate to meet. To top it off, we were treated to a picnic at the Cannstatter-Volksfest-Verein, a huge meadow on the outskirts of Philadelphia. It was a memorable day. The sun was shining, the band was playing, people of all ages were dancing, addresses and stories were swapped, and at intervals the choirs were singing. The food was good and plentiful, and the beer was cold and free. What else can a human being ask for?

Thanks to all the participants who worked so hard to make this event a success.

I'd like to add a little verse that I repeat many times in situations of stress.

Allen Gewalten zum Trotz sich erhalten, nimmer sich beugen, mutig sich zeigen, das rufet die Arme der Goetter herbei.

Against all forces remain steadfast; do not bend, show courage, and the arms of the Gods will support you.

An appeal to the German American community

(Published in the <GermanAmericanPioneer.org>
Web site newsletter, July 2006)

Thought for the month. Ohne eine innere Verbindung zu unsererHeimat wuerden wir verarmen, es schwer haben uns in der Gegenwart zu orientieren und eine Perspective fuer die Zukunft zu gewinnen. - Karl Karsten, Bundespresident Deutschlands.

Without an inner connection to our ancestors, we are impoverished; we will feel lost in the here and now and have difficulty to find a sense of direction for the future.

A couple of weeks ago I received my **Spring- Summer** newsletter from the "**United German American Committee,**" a nationwide umbrella organization for German American clubs in the USA, in short UGAC. This organization concerns itself with many subjects and programs regarding the German American community. The one program that stands out and should be of interest to all of us is the **German American Museum in Washington DC.**

I have been a member of UGAC for several years and know some of the men and women on the board personally. I know they are committed, dedicated and concerned German Americans, who spend much of their time and money working tirelessly to make the vision of having a German American Museum or Heritage Center a reality.

All of them are successful businessmen who have the know-how and determination to achieve this goal.

Yet, we cannot expect them to build the Museum totally on their own; they need our help. They need members and they need money. I have often heard the expression, "In my heart I will always be a German." I think it is high time we do something for our heart and get in touch with UGAC, learn about their plans and their accomplishments.

It has been almost 400 years since the first Germans arrived in Virginia. In 2006, we are still the largest ethnic group in this country. Our people have done their share in building this nation, making it the strongest country on earth.

I came after World War II like most of the German immigrants who have now reached retirement age. The only wealth we brought to this land of **unlimited opportunities** was our heritage, and this heritage has served us well.

It was our upbringing, the Kinderstube, that sustained us, encouraged us to do our best and ask for no handout. This is a way of life, drummed into us in the homeland. It helped us to become contributing citizens and achieve one of the highest standards of living anywhere. In the 50 years I have lived in this country, I have not met one German immigrant on welfare. Most of us live very comfortable; many of us travel, not only to Germany but travel to see the world.

"We worked for it, we are entitled to it", I hear my landsmen reply.

I will say, "Yes, go for it, but let's not neglect our duty to preserve our heritage for our children and grandchildren." The face of America, as we know it, is changing. We can no longer take for granted that practically everything we look at and are surrounded by has a European background. People speak of a **Cultural War.** How do we preserve the heritage of the **heart of Europe, the German speaking nations** in this country for future generations? Our descendents can benefit by following the role models our ancestors have established. How better can we show them than to work on a museum to preserve this source of strength for them in this multicultural society?

Over the centuries Germans brought skills to this country, which were not yet introduced here. They came from Central Europe where all the trade routes crossed. The Germans were privileged to find themselves in that position, to exchange ideas and goods with their many neighbors.

When they came to the new world they applied this know-how; built workshops and taught others. Much of what they contributed is still visible. We can stand in awe looking at their masterful work. We know it will never be taught in schools. **It is up to us to make it available to future generations.** Our descendents can draw from all this and get inspired by it. The Government does not do it for us. We cannot expect the other ethnic groups to do it for us. They do it for themselves and so must we.

This is the only "Heimat" our descendent will ever know. We, the immigrants, can always fly to good old Germany and reconnect with the past. We come back refreshed and go about our daily routine. Our descendents also need a place where they can connect to their past. **A museum is the place.** Das Elternhaus (homestead) in most cases will have been sold or even razed. It will not be there for them to visit and even the cemetery has taken on a new and different meaning. The ashes of a loved one might have been strewn in the forest or at sea and might wash ashore by the waves of the oceans. Look around you and you will have to agree that the need to belong is great.

I believe it is our duty to preserve our rich heritage for our children. Yes, we had at one time beautiful clubhouses, concert halls, churches and meeting places. Yes, most of it was lost on account of the two wars in the twentieth century. We do not have to accept this condition as final. Most of us are fairly well off. We can make a contribution to the **Hockemeier Hall in Washington DC** and make it into a **Museum and Heritage Center for all German Americans**

living now and for future generations. Remember, the last shirt has no pockets.

Since we live in the computer age and I live in Silicon Valley, I like to include a few Emails I received and my reply.

Can a Muslim be a good American?

(E-mail sent to me by a friend during the Obama campaign.)

My friend writes:
I sent that question to a friend who worked in Saudi Arabia for twenty years. The following is his reply:

Theologically—no. Because his allegiance is to Allah, the moon god of Arabia.

Religiously—no. Because no other religion is accepted by his Allah except Islam (Qumran, 2:256)

Scripturally—no. Because his allegiance is to the five pillars of Islam and the Qumran (Koran).

Geographically—no. Because his allegiance is to Mecca, to which he turns in prayer five times a day.

Socially—no. Because his allegiance to Islam forbids him to make friends with Christians or Jews.

Politically—no. Because he must submit to the mullah (spiritual leaders), who teach annihilation of Israel and the destruction of America, the great Satan.

Domestically—no. Because he is instructed to marry four women and beat and scourge his wives when they disobey him (Qumran 4:34).

Intellectually—no. Because he cannot accept the American Constitution since it is based on biblical principles, and he believes the Bible to be corrupt.

Philosophically—no. Because Islam, Muhammad, and the Qumran do not allow freedom of religion and expression. Democracy and Islam cannot coexist. Every Muslim government is either dictatorial or autocratic.

Spiritually—no. Because when we declare "one nation under God," the Christian's God is loving and kind, while Allah is NEVER referred to as heavenly father, nor is he ever called love in the Qumran's 99 excellent names.

Therefore after much study and deliberation ... perhaps we should be very suspicious of ALL MUSLIMS in this country. They obviously cannot be both "good" Muslims and good Americans.
Call it what you wish ... it's still the truth.

If you find yourself intellectually in agreement with the above statements, perhaps you will share this with your friends. The more who understand this, the better it will be for our country and for our future.
Pass it on, fellow Americans. The religious war is bigger than we know or understand.

My reply

I do not agree with you or with your friend who lived in Saudi Arabia. I do not want to live in fear, nor do I want to hate.

In the fifty years I have lived in the United States it has been suggested to hate different groups and nationalities at different times for different reasons, but the most evil of them all are still the Nazis, as can be witnessed on TV and the media in general every day.

Since the noble Allies slammed the collective guilt on all Germans, all Germans have had to pay and are still paying in one form or another, for crimes committed by relatively few. I do not believe that even the United States has the capacity or the will to be fair, but rather is opportunistic.

Every school teaches about the evil Germans. I find them to be as decent as any other people, and that includes the "American born-again Christians". How can I trust a country that does not face up to war crimes committed by its own people? Why does America refuse to admit that more than twelve thousand Germans were interned in this country along with the Japanese and Italians during World War II?

Where is the justice when an eighty-nine-year old man is expelled from this country for having been a guard at a concentration camp when he was very young? Sixty years of exemplary living does not make up for a relatively short time spent as a guard—very Christian like.

Is he guiltier than the leaders of the Allied forces, who signed the papers to expel twelve to fifteen million Germans from the eastern parts of Europe, where they had lived for hundreds of years? They knew very well that the only place they could go was to a bombed-out Germany, and all this took place in the middle of winter. That was very Christian like.

Are the Muslims trying to protect their lifestyle? Yes. Are they afraid of us, as we are of them? Are we better than they? I have not seen it yet. We just have to ask who is bombing whom? How many civilians have been killed besides our people on 9/11, not counting the soldiers on both sides? Who wants to dominate whom? My mother was right when she said, "Mein Nachbars Teufel is so viel schwaerzer als mein Teufel." (My neighbor's devil is so much blacker than mine own).

Since when are you such a Christian, Joe? Wo ist dein Gottvertrauen? (Where is your trust in God?)

"O, mein Christ lass Gott nur walten, seine Lieb wacht immer fort. Seine Hand wird treu dich halten, wahr und heilig ist sein Wort."

Translation: "Dear Christians, let the Lord rule; his love will keep watch; he will hold your hand; his word is holy like it is truthful."

Do I believe all that? Not really, but I do not believe that Christians will behave in a Godlike manner when the pressure is on and neither will the Muslims.

My observation has been that one is not much different from the other. We are all human. I believe in the Golden Rule: "Do on to others as you would want them to do on to you."

Maybe, that is naïve too, but the American rule as it applies to the Iraqi war, "Do unto them before they do it to you," has been tried and does not work.

I sleep well at night, knowing the world is a dangerous place. Maybe we are lucky and will slip through unharmed. Who knows?

Have a good day. Pass it on to other fellow Americans.

All the BEST,
Maria

Another subject I like to mention is gay marriage

How do I feel about gay marriage? Since this is such a sensitive issue at this time in history, I will give my thoughts on the subject honestly. Marriage is a sacrament, or so we were taught, but who lives up to it?

People get divorced at all ages and at any time, sometimes more than once. In other words, few people seem to take marriage seriously, few believe it is for life. Yet, these same people vehemently oppose gay marriage.

I was married for forty-five years when my husband died, and I wished we would have had another ten years or so together. We had gay friends who were very decent people and often went out of their way to do good for others. Their lifestyle did, in no way, interfere with ours. Why should I deny them the right to get married? I voted to legalize gay marriage the last time it was on the ballot in California. Live and let live is my motto. People will change their mind when a taboo becomes popular. Gay marriage is definitely such a taboo. The path will be smoothed, but it will still take some time.

On taking Christ out of Christmas

During the month of December 2008 I received at least five of these letters by e-mail from different parts of the United States. People are afraid that Christ will be taken out of Christmas. A copy of the letter and my response will follow.

MERRY CHRISTMAS!!!

It was the month before Christmas
When all through our land,
Not a Christian was praying
Nor taking a stand.
See the PC Police had taken away,
The reason for Christmas - no one could say.
The children were told by their schools not to sing,
About Shepherds and Wise Men and Angels and things.
It might hurt people's feelings, the teachers would say
* December 25th is just a "Holiday ".*

Yet the shoppers were ready with cash, checks and credit
Pushing folks down to the floor just to get it!
CDs from Madonna, an X BOX, an I-pod
*Something was changing, something quite odd! *
Retailers promoted Ramadan and Kwanzaa

In hopes to sell books by Franken & Fonda.
As Targets were hanging their trees upside down
* At Lowe's the word Christmas - was nowhere to be found.*
At K-Mart and Staples and Penny's and Sears
You won't hear the word Christmas; it won't touch your ears.

Inclusive, sensitive, Di-ver-is-ty
Are words that were used to intimidate me.
Now Daschle, Now Darden, Now Sharpton, Wolf Blitzen
On Boxer, on Rather, on Kerry, on Clinton !
At the top of the Senate, there arose such a clatter
To eliminate Jesus, in all public matter.
And we spoke not a word, as they took away our faith
* Forbidden to speak of salvation and grace*

The true Gift of Christmas was exchanged and discarded
The reason for the season, stopped before it started.
So as you celebrate "Winter Break" under your "Dream Tree"
Sipping your Starbucks, listen to me.
Choose your words carefully, choose what you say

*Shout MERRY CHRISTMAS,
Not Happy Holiday!*

My response

I like this type of talk very much.

I believe that something can only be taken away if it exists. The meaning of Christmas has not existed for a long, long time. Christians have not followed, nor have they tried to live up to Christ's teaching. Who follows the teaching of the "Sermon on the Mount"? Christ is not their God. Money is. That is what everyone seems to believe; Christians are no exception.

That is the purpose for people to get a good education, so they can make much money to buy much stuff, which in the long run might weigh them down. The kingdom of heaven is on earth; at least that is how it is expressed in practically every lifestyle in this Silicon Valley. Having much stuff is heaven for most people. This is not new. Not a person or religion mentioned in this poem has had the will to change this lifestyle. We brought this upon ourselves.

If anything, the other religions or ethnic groups have forced us to look in the mirror to examine our behavior. The Christians have been kidding themselves all along. It was so comforting to live in a fantasy world. We were sure we were right and so much better than most of the others.

There are very few Christians who believe that, "Whatever you do to the least of my brothers, that you do onto me. Love thy neighbor as thyself." When Jesus was asked in the temple, "Who is thy brother or neighbor?" he answered: "Everyone." That includes people who are not like us. Jesus was a troublemaker who upset the whole conservative society of his time. He was a liberal and a revolutionary; some might even say he was a socialist. He made his fellow citizens, who were so sure of themselves and of their goodness, uncomfortable. And for that he was nailed to the cross and paid with his life. If he walked the streets today it would not be any different.

I wonder how he would grade the Christians of the Western World today. I think he might take the whip and chase them out of the church and politics like he did with the Pharisees.

This is how I see it. I think Christ would be busy slapping us around. He might even give preferential treatment to the others, of whom we are afraid, and turn his back on us. He even demanded we love our enemy. Being a Christian is hard work. That is why I hesitate to call myself a Christian. I am not sure that I want to or can live up to such a tough command.

Will we be rewarded in the afterlife? No one knows for sure. Try your best and let the chips fall but let's not blame others for our shortcomings.

On immigration

This "letter to the editor" was sent to me by friends from the East- as well as the West Coast. It is in regards to legal and illegal immigration. The letter states how the immigrants of previous generations came here, kissed the ground, forgot their mother tongue and became instant Americans in their daily life.

My response follows:

Being an immigrant myself, I felt I had to respond, especially since the subject is very current and controversial and has been on my mind more than once.

Thanks for sending the letter. I will not forward the letter as was requested. I do not agree with most of the statements the lady made. The rosy picture she is trying to convey of the immigrants of previous generations is an American myth and has little to do with how things really were. It is easy to distort the facts, but even American history, like it or not, was and is at times quite ugly.

Not everyone who came to this country was happy to be here. Many immigrants could not wait to return to the country of their birth and left these shores at their first opportunity.

People did not respect each other's culture, and America was not a melting pot. Newspaper ads would state: "Irish need not apply."

During the First World War, Germans were hanged and their businesses were destroyed and books were burned even though Germans had contributed to this country since 1608, one year after Jamestown was founded and twelve years before the Mayflower arrived.

The situation was not much better during the Second World War. Japanese, German, and Italian legal immigrants and citizens were interned and their properties confiscated. These (so good) Americans did nothing to prevent the authorities from sending their neighbors to concentration camps. These Americans were as guilty as their German counterparts, who did nothing when the Jews were picked up and their properties destroyed or confiscated. The difference is the Germans are still paying for not intervening, sixty years later. They pay financially and emotionally while the self-righteous Americans preach about human decency and equality and justice for all.

The black men, who joined the armed forces and put their lives on the line for this country, still did not have equal rights when they returned after the war. They could not sit at the same counter or swim in the same pool with their white neighbors. Some of the black-men, as well as some Filipinos did not receive their medal of honor until sixty years after earning it.

Where were their Anglo American comrades, who represented the "greatest generation," when their minority fellow soldiers needed them?

Immigrants of the nineteenth century wanted to be Americans and denied everything that reminded them of their old country, the woman states. That is a joke. A person did not then and cannot now enter the United States as an immigrant, peel off his or her culture, religion, and background to become an American instantly.

Life is like a pyramid. We build one layer on top of the other and mature in the process. One cannot just forget about his upbringing and culture on demand. Everyone's foundation goes back to his childhood, regardless what continent the person calls home.

What makes an American? An American is a person who took advantage of this vast land and its natural resources. These offered him enormous opportunities to become an independent person, who at times accumulated enormous wealth. The skills and culture he had brought with him were the tools and often his only assets to achieve lofty goal.

The immigrant did not become an Indian—a real American. He clung to his culture. In fact, the missionaries came to impose the European faith and culture on the original inhabitants, and they and their fellow Europeans brutally eliminated a whole people.

The European immigrant of the nineteenth century lived his culture to the fullest. I know that the German machinist, for example, often spoke German at work. When work was done he went home to his German village, where his wife had prepared a German meal, for which she had bought the ingredients in a German market. Even the children went to German American schools, and on Sundays they all listened to a German sermon in a church that had German architecture. At times they would visit a German Biergarten in the afternoon.

This was no different for an Italian, Irish, or Greek immigrant. Most of them found happiness by spending at least their leisure time with their own people, speaking their mother tongue

"America is a beacon to the world," the lady writes. I would question that very much, especially at this particular time in history. America still has the power and is eager to show its power to the world. Is this how we want every nation and community to live? Has man progressed so little that we can only live by the laws of nature, where the stronger will win and survive? America started out and built a nation by the people and for the people. If we had tried to live up to that promise, we could actually be the beacon to the world the lady is talking about.

But Americans chose to get involved in conflicts around the world and lately has created the conflict. I believe the motive was and is greed and a hunger to be the world power. I believe greed will eventually destroy us.

Immigration of Latino and Oriental people

A Latino or Oriental immigrant will learn to love this country and become a good American just like the Europeans became good Americans. He too will need his culture to sustain him, just like the Europeans did. Taking his native culture away from him is cruel; it means taking away his foundation, which, in most cases, is his source of his strength. Once the foundation is removed, the immigrant finds himself on shaky ground. That has been my observation.

Let him have his culture. Give him time for transition. It will be better for him and for this country. Most likely he will become a person living in both cultures even after many decades. His children will eagerly embrace the American culture without us forcing it on them.

The so called Anglo Americans are still following the religions and culture of their European ancestors some four hundred years later.

Let's be patient and reasonable with our new immigrants. Does the "pursuit of happiness" guaranteed to every American not apply to our new citizens? Let them speak their mother tongue. They themselves will realize that English will help them to achieve the American dream sooner.

I am sure the lady who wrote the **"Letter to the Editor"** has never earned a living in a foreign country, where she had to learn another language and try to fit in among total strangers.

I have observed the American traveler (my family and myself included) hurrying to the first McDonald's we see while visiting a foreign country, just to catch a taste of our American culture, or, one might say, a taste of home. I have learned to love this country deeply, but I still live in two worlds even more than fifty years after I immigrated.

PS: As far as illegal immigration is concerned, let's punish the people who hire them. Many of my friends complain bitterly about the illegal workers who pay no taxes but most of them pay their cleaning woman in cash.

All the best to you always.

Letter to the editor and my reply

A German immigrant by the name of Alfred, living in Canada, wrote a letter to the editor of the New York Staats Zeitung in response to a letter favorable to Ernst Zuendel.

Who is Ernst Zuendel? Ernst is a man who is also a German immigrant living in Canada and who is one of the very few people worldwide who dare question some aspects of the Holocaust. Because he voiced his opinion openly, Ernst is now living in a prison in Germany.

Alfred apparently could not comprehend that there are people in this world who speak their mind regardless of consequences. He sent a hateful but political correct letter to the editor. Alfred's letter was published in the New Yorker Staats Zeitung November 2005.

"My blood pressure rose," he wrote. Alfred's hateful slurs went like this: "This man is an embarrassment to the good German Canadians and he (Alfred) is ashamed to be of the same generation as Ernst Zuendel and it pains him to share the same heritage." He cannot say enough about this "ignorant, mean-spirited, and ordinary inciter of hate speech." Alfred cannot contain his pleasure, knowing that Ernst is now finally behind bars.

When I read his letter, my blood pressure rose also, and I had to respond.

My letter below was published in the Staatszeitung in December 2005:

December 2005

My response to "Meinung" (opinion)
I feel pity for Mr. Alfred. What upsets this poor soul is the fact that there are people among us who dare to go against the establishment. Alfred believes in obeying the law, regardless what the law stands for. I don't know if Alfred is old enough to have lived during the time of the Third Reich. If he did, I am sure he played it safe and did nothing to improve the conditions of the Jewish people, the same people he now so vehemently defends. The situation has changed, and it is safer to be on their side.

What is wrong with this? In both cases the law did not then and does not now apply equally to all citizens, and that is the crime.

It was dangerous then as it is now for individuals to stand up and demand equal and humane treatment under the law for all citizens. Mr. Zuendel and his wife have experienced this fact on many occasions.

Mr. and Mrs. Zuendel are in good company and can draw strength from all these great personalities who have left their mark on history and made this world a better place. Jesus Christ changed the world drastically, and so did Martin Luther, George Washington, Thomas Jefferson, Gandi, Dr. Martin Luther King, and Friedrich Schiller, just to name a few.

All of them had one thing in common; all worked against the establishment. They followed their conscience. All of them "ran where the brave dared not go," as is stated in the song: The impossible dream. Not one of them closed their eyes to the unequal and unfair treatment of his fellow man.

I admire Mr. and Mrs. Zuendel; I have supported Mr. Zuendel financially. I do not see myself as a radical or an anti-Semite. I can and will not follow the law blindly. I question the motives of a government; I grow extremely skeptical when I am forbidden by law to express my opinion openly after I have researched a subject, spent much time weighing the issue, and reached certain conclusions.

German people have had to endure emotional abuse during most of the twentieth century, and it does not seem to stop in the twenty-first century. The media never tires of calling them derogatory names. People in Germany do not only have to deal with the emotional abuse, but they are also being forced to pay part of their earnings for crimes they never committed.

What is it that Mr. Zuendel is being jailed for? Mr. Zuendel asks the question: Did six million Jews really die? I believe it is a fair question, and he should be allowed to ask it.

On December 26, 1994, the *Mercury News*, a daily paper in San Jose, California, published the article "Camp's future debated as anniversary nears." The camp is Auschwitz. Here is a quote: "A year after Poland's communist government collapsed in 1989, the curators at Auschwitz removed the plaque that had claimed 4 million dead."

Somewhat further into the story it states: "How best to honor the 1.1million to 1.5 million people who died here."

Is Tom Hundley, who wrote the story, questioning the facts as they are dictated to the German people in jail for spreading lies about the Holocaust? I guess not.

This is just one story. There are many others, all saying that the six million number is exaggerated. All these brave people, including rabbis, say what Zuendel is saying. Is the Holocaust a money-making scheme? I believe it is.

Let the facts speak for themselves. The truth will set all of us free, but it might break the "Holocaust bank."

As long as there are laws preventing open discussion on a subject that affects so many people, I tend to follow my own instinct, whether the result of doing so is factual or not. I do not want to be told what I can or cannot believe.

To condemn a whole people as war criminals is also an unforgiving crime against humanity. The slogan "Never again," should definitely apply here.

No other ethnic group has ever been burdened with such a stigma, even though cruelties have occurred throughout the ages, committed by and endured by all kinds of people. I find the German people to be as decent as any other people on this earth. Why, then, should they suffer this inhuman emotional abuse?

Since this fact never seems to bother any of the leaders of the victorious countries, I place no trust in their judgment. I know what I know and believe what I believe.

As for Alfred, I can only say, it is a man's will to sacrifice for the sake of justice that sets him apart from other creatures. That is the difference between a man and a mouse. I leave it up to the readers to place the two men, Mr. Zuendel and Mr. Alfred, into the right category.

I hope the Zuendels have a pleasant holiday season in spite of the treatment they have to endure. I wish them good health and much success in the coming year.

Here is a fitting verse for Mr. Alfred:

Die Gedanken sind frei, wagst du sie zu sprechen?
Deinen Geist und Verstand wird man versuchen zu brechen.
Man wird dich verdammen, nicht ruhn dich auszuspannen.
Willst populaer du sein, trag als Herdenvieh dich ein.

MB

Translated by Maria Brand.

Your thoughts are your own.
Do you dare give them a voice?
You will be condemned for doing so.
They will try to break your spirit.
If you want to be popular,
Be a sheep and follow blindly.

Letters and responses to and from people in Government and others

Letter to President Clinton on behalf of Dr. Arthur Rudolph

March 20, 1993

Dear Mr. President,

My name is Maria Brand. I came to this country in 1956 and became a United States Citizen in 1968. I am writing on behalf of Dr. Arthur Rudolph who was exiled from this country in 1984.

Dr. Rudolph came with Dr. Werner von Braun shortly after World War II, to work on the American Space Program.

As head of the American Rocket Program his contribution was paramount in landing an American on the Moon. During his 40 years of service to this country he gave his knowledge, his energy, his loyalty for this country. After he had outlived his usefulness he was discarded like an old shoe.

The "Office of Special Investigation" accused him of crimes against humanity, during the Second World War. Knowing he did not have the funds, or the physical strength to defend himself against the "Office of Special Investigation" he left this country, never to be allowed to return again.

Mr. Rudolph is now 89 years old. His time as well as his money is running out.

I am asking you, Mr. President, to intervene on his behalf. I do not know whom I can turn to.

I have never met Dr. Rudolph. He is just another old person, yet it hurts me to know that he is suffering. I cannot see the justice in not allowing him to visit the United States of America, to visit his only daughter.

Mr. President, I believe you are a fair-minded, compassioned person, I have faith in you.

Thank you,
Maria Brand

Letter from the White House

THE WHITE HOUSE
WASHINGTON

June 5, 1993

Mrs. Maria Brand
8691 Lomas Azules Place
San Jose, California 95135

Dear Mrs. Brand:

Thank you so much for your letter. President Clinton greatly appreciates the trust and confidence you have expressed in him by writing.

To give your concerns the special attention they deserve, the President has asked me to forward your letter to the Department of State. I have asked them to provide you with a prompt reply, but please bear in mind that it may take several weeks to look thoroughly into the concerns you have raised. Should you have any questions after reviewing their response to you, you may write: Department of State, 2201 C Street, N.W., Washington, D.C. 20520.

Many thanks for your patience.

Sincerely,

Marsha Scott
Deputy Assistant to the President
Director of Correspondence and
Presidential Messages

United States Department of State

Washington, D.C. 20520

June 21, 1993

Ms. Maria Brand
8691 Lomas Azules Place
San Jose, California 95135

Dear Ms. Brand:

The White House has referred to us for reply your letter of March 20 concerning the nonimmigrant visa case of Dr. Arthur Rudolph.

I understand your concerns about Dr. Rudolph. However, he has been found ineligible for a visa under Section 212(a)(3)(E)(i) of the Immigration and Nationality Act cited in the enclosure. This section of the law prohibits the issuance of a visa to anyone who participated in the persecution of any person because of race, religion, national origin, or political opinion during the period from March 23, 1933 to May 8, 1945, under the direction of or in association with the Nazi government of Germany, or an occupied government. There is no provision in the law for a waiver of this ground of ineligibility.

Sincerely,

Ron Acker
Deputy Director,
Office of Public and
Diplomatic Liaison
Visa Services

Enclosure:
    DSL 851

I have never met Dr. Arthur Rudolph, but could not bear the way he was treated by the American government and press, now that he was old and sick. Had he not given his knowledge, energy, and goodwill to the space program? He had been a key person in landing an American on the moon. Now that he was old, America remembered that he had entered the country illegally, conveniently forgetting that he and the others were brought here under a special program, called "Paper Clip." He had served their purpose. It was OK to discard him now like an old shoe.

I have to say, the members of the "Office of Special Investigation," a Jewish organization has learned their lessons well. I believe OSI is certainly capable of surpassing the Nazis in every way.

Letter from Dr. Arthur Rudolph

```
Arthur Rudolph                    Classenweg 50
                                  DW-2000 Hamburg 65
                                  Germany
                                  11. Mai 1991
```

Sehr geehrte, liebe Frau Brand,

Herzlichsten Dank für Ihren lieben Brief vom 23.4.91, und der Beilage "Brief an 60 Minutes". Ich bewundere Sie und Ihren Mann für die Zeit und Energie die Sie zur Unterstützung des Deutschtums und für mich ,aufbringen. Hoffentlich sehen Sie einen Erfolg Ihrer Arbeit. Ich und auch meine Frau wünschen es von ganzem Herzen.

Nochmals herzlichen Dank für Ihre selbstlose, grossartige Unterstützung.

Mit allen guten Wünschen für Ihr ferneres Wohlergehen und viel Erfolg in allem was Sie unternehmen .

Herzlichst,

Ihr

Art Rudolph u. Frau Martha

Arthur Rudolph und Frau Martha

I have collected and contributed money for the Old Timers Fund, an organization to help finance the defense of Arthur Rudolph and others of the original "Paper Clip" men, should they ever need it. I have written letters to senators and members of congress, to newspapers and organizations which I thought could help Rudolph. I have many replies from the above mentioned, as well as letters from the German rocket scientists themselves. This is just one letter, and since it is short I do want to translate it. I recommend a book called *An American in Exile: The Story of Arthur Rudolph,* by Thomas Franklin.

Translation of the Letter from Dr. Rudolph:

Dear Mrs. Brand

A heartfelt thank you for the letter dated April 23, 1991 and the copy of a memo you mailed to 60 Minutes on my behalf. I admire you and your husband for the time and energy you spend in support of our German Heritage and for me personally. I sincerely hope that you will be rewarded for all the work. This, my wife and I hope for with all our hearts.

Again, thank you for your self-less, and enormous support.

With best wishes for your future welfare and much success in everything you undertake.
Sincerely - Art Rudolph and Mrs. Martha

Letter to Congressman Norman Mineta

Dear Mr. Mineta,

I like to thank you with all my heart for coming to the Geramania Hall and help us celebrate our anniversary. Your appearance gave us the much needed ray of light to warm our hearts. The German immigrants, even though financially secure and often prosperous, suffer in silence.

For more than 40 years we have been emotionally bashed or ignored. One never gets quite used to it and it still hurts.-

I know your people are suffering the same faith. I am sending you a small book called "The Gruesome Harvest." I know it is the truth; we lived through it. I am sure your people have their own story.

History means "His Story." To improve the world situation we must be allowed to learn the full story. Yet, in the United States of America, a nation of immigrants, history is taught selectively to the American public in a distorted manner, totally out of context.

I hope the citizens of the United States will hurry and pay reparations to the Japanese Americans as promised, before the victims have passed away. How else can we speak of Liberty and Justice for all Americans.

We can never make good but, we can say, we are sorry.

Thank you,
Sincerely – Maria Brand

PS: At the time I wrote this letter, I did not know that German and Italian legal immigrants as well as some citizens were interned also.

One would think that Mineta, as an elected representative, would have tried to get justice for all victims, but he chose to take care of his own kind only.

NORMAN Y. MINETA
MEMBER OF CONGRESS
13TH DISTRICT, CALIFORNIA

DEPUTY WHIP

COMMITTEES:
PUBLIC WORKS AND
TRANSPORTATION
SUBCOMMITTEE ON SURFACE TRANSPORTATION
CHAIRMAN

SCIENCE, SPACE, AND TECHNOLOGY

Congress of the United States
House of Representatives
Washington, DC 20515

WASHINGTON OFFICE:
2350 RAYBURN HOUSE OFFICE BUILDING
WASHINGTON, DC 20515
TELEPHONE (202) 225-2631

DISTRICT OFFICE:
SUITE 310
1245 SOUTH WINCHESTER BOULEVARD
SAN JOSE, CA 95128-3963
TELEPHONE (408) 984-6045

February 22, 1990

Ms. Maria Brand
1338 Elsona Dr.
Sunnyvale, California 94087

Dear Maria:

I was pleased to receive your letter and the book, "The Gruesome Harvest." Although this response is delayed, it does not lessen my appreciation to your kindness.

The book will serve as a constant reminder of the unfair treatment and prejudice many immigrants in the U.S. experienced during WWII and still experience today. I believe that it is of utmost importance that Americans realize the wrongdoing enacted on certain U.S. citizens during the war. In being reminded of the emotional pain and suffering we have inflicted upon them, we will ensure that acts such as the internment of Asian Americans never happen again.

I want to extend my gratitude to you for allowing me to share the 80th anniversary of your organization. I wish you all the best in your future endeavors.

Warmest regards,

NORMAN Y. MINETA
Member of Congress

NYM:cap.i

PS: "**The Gruesome Harvest, an Attempt to Exterminate the People of Germany**" is a book dealing with World War II and its aftermath, written by the American Ralph Franklin Keeling in 1947. It is a very important book, that every German and German -American should read, especially the younger generation.

Available at Amazon, Very good.

Letter to Congressman Paul N. McCloskey Jr.

(In 1986, I wrote a letter to then Congressman Paul McCloskey Jr. I wrote it by hand on a yellow pad because I did not know how to type at the time. This is what it said.)

Dear Mr. McCloskey,

For 40 years I supported the Jewish Community in word and deed. All this changed during the Bitburg fiasco. I grew skeptical.

This feeling was reinforced with the expulsion of Dr. Arthur Rudolph. It grew to resentment and sadness during the vicious attacks on Dr. Waldheim when he was campaigning for the presidency of Austria.

I am reading the book "They Dare to Speak Out" by Paul Findley. It did not open my eyes but confirmed what I already knew. For centuries, Christians all over the world have used the Crucifixion of Christ as a reason, as well as an excuse, to persecute, incriminate, defame, disown, use as scapegoats and kill the Jewish people to further their own agenda.

All this was done with the total conviction of doing what was right.

In the second half of the twentieth century the Jewish people are walking that same path. They use the "Holocaust" as a reason as well as an excuse to persecute, incriminate, defame, disown, use as scapegoats and kill people to further their own agenda.

All this is done with the total conviction of doing what is right.

The motives for both persecutions are the same, greed and an obsession to dominate the world. The outcome will also be the same.

The difference is all the free world is financing the second Holocaust, mostly the taxpayers of the United States and the people of Germany. The German people pay vast sums of money to Israel and the Jewish people abroad through their Retribution Programs. The German ethnic group is the largest in the United States. The majority belong to the Middle Class. It is well known that this segment of society pays the most taxes. Most of the German people enjoy to work; few ever collect welfare.

Wake up America. Let's elect representatives who are not puppets of the "American-Israeli-Public-Affairs Committee" or any other PAC. AIPAC is a Rat Pac.

"Holocaust" stands for: "Haggle over lots of cash at unaccountable, scrupulous Tel Aviv."

This is the conclusion I have reached totally on my own and I am just a house wife.

Thank you,
Sincerely - Maria Brand

BROBECK, PHLEGER & HARRISON

SAN FRANCISCO OFFICE
SPEAR STREET TOWER
ONE MARKET PLAZA
SAN FRANCISCO, CALIFORNIA 94105
(415) 442-0900

ATTORNEYS AT LAW
TWO EMBARCADERO PLACE
2200 GENG ROAD
PALO ALTO, CALIFORNIA 94303
FACSIMILE: (415) 496-2885
TELEX: WUI 6771160 BPH UW WUD 34226 BPH SFO
CABLE ADDRESS: BROBECK
TELEPHONE: (415) 424-0160

LOS ANGELES OFFICE
444 SOUTH FLOWER STREET
LOS ANGELES, CALIFORNIA 90017
(213) 489-4060

September 2, 1986

Mr. W. Brand
1338 Elsona Drive
Sunnyvale, CA 94087

Dear Mr. Brand:

Thank you for your letter. Here is an extra copy of "They Dare to Speak Out" to give to a friend.

All the best,

Paul N. McCloskey, Jr.

PNMcC:kap

Enclosure

Congressman McCloskey lost his reelection because he confronted Israel's lobby. The book *They Dare to Speak Out*, by Paul Findley, (mentioned above) deals with the very subject of America's pro-Israeli lobby (AIPAC). It is an eye-opener.

Letter from Senator Dianne Feinstein

DIANNE FEINSTEIN
CALIFORNIA

COMMITTEE ON APPROPRIATIONS
COMMITTEE ON THE JUDICIARY
COMMITTEE ON RULES AND ADMINISTRATION

United States Senate
WASHINGTON, DC 20510-0504

February 18, 1994

Mr. and Mrs. Walter Brand
8691 Lomas Azules Place
San Jose, California 95135

Dear Mr. and Mrs. Brand:

Thank you for contacting me regarding the case of John Demjanjuk. I appreciate hearing from you.

As you may know, John Demjanjuk has returned to the United States after having been extradited to Israel to stand trial for war crimes as the alleged Nazi death camp guard "Ivan the Terrible". The Israeli court determined that Mr. Demjanjuk was not guilty of the crimes for which he was charged and subsequently deported.

There have been some questions regarding the Justice Department's handling of the case. As a result, the U.S. Court of Appeals in Cincinnati appointed a judge to investigate and determine whether proper procedures were followed in John Demjanjuk's extradition to Israel. The final report on this case is expected in the months to come. Be assured that I will continue to monitor this matter as it progresses.

Again, thank you for writing. If you have any future concerns or questions, do not hesitate to contact me. Please know that I am working hard to represent the best interests of California in the Senate.

Sincerely,

Dianne Feinstein
United States Senator

DF:jej

John Demjanjuk was a guard at a concentration camp in Romania during World War II. This year, 2009, at the age of 89, being old and sick, he was deported to stand trial in Munich, Germany. Never mind that he, like everyone serving his country, followed orders. He was very young and lived under a dictatorship at the time of his "crime." For decades, he lived an exemplary life in the United States. Germany ordered his extradition and America complied.

Shame on both countries while at the same time the officials who ordered and committed torture at Guantanamo Bay and elsewhere are free to enjoy life as usual. This is what is called "Equal Justice to all."

Letter from Senator Cranston

ALAN CRANSTON
CALIFORNIA

United States Senate
WASHINGTON, DC 20510

July 8, 1985

Ms. Maria Brand
1338 Elsona Drive
Sunnyvale, California 94087

Dear Ms. Brand,

Thank you for your letter about President Reagan's visit to the military cemetery at Bitburg.

I do not think the President of the United States should have gone to a German cemetery to honor Nazi soldiers who died in the service of the greatest tyrant of all times, Adolf Hitler. The choice of the Bitburg cemetery as a site to commemorate reconciliation with the German people was extremely unfortunate and insensitive. I am dismayed about the terrible memories and the pain this visit unleashed.

Because I felt so strongly about this matter, I authored a resolution, S. Con. Res. 42, urging the President to reconsider and to cancel his proposed visit to Bitburg. The Senate passed a modified version of my resolution, which asked the President to reassess his itinerary for his visit to the Federal Republic of Germany.

I also joined a number of my Senate colleagues in a letter to President Reagan asking him not to go to Bitburg. The letter suggested that a more appropriate gesture of reconciliation be found and that congratulating the German people in their great accomplishments of the past 40 years did not preclude memorializing the millions of innocent victims of the Nazi regime who died in the Holocaust.

Because of your concern, I am sending you a copy of the statement I made on the Senate floor while the Bitburg resolution was under consideration, and a copy of S. Con. Res. 42, the resolution I authored.

I very much appreciated hearing from you on this issue.

Sincerely,

Alan Cranston

Enclosures

Letter from Dr. Don Heinrich Tolzmann

18 August 1994

Dear Mrs. Brand,

Thank you for your recent card with your work on the Turnverein. I think you have done an excellent job with the Turner work, and I am going to send information about it to the Society for German-American Studies Newsletter! I was not aware that there were so many Turnvereine in California.

Also, many thanks for the work you have done in distributing brochures - should you ever need more, pls. let me know. Also, thank you for your kind words with regard to my work!

Sincerely,

Dr. Don Heinrich Tolzmann
Blegen Library M.L. 113
University of Cincinnati
Cincinnati, Oh. 45221

PS: I had compiled a book about the Turner Movement in San Jose, Sacramento, and the San Francisco Bay Area. The San Jose Turners introduced physical education into the public schools in 1891. The Turner Club in San Jose was founded in 1868.

The principles of the society are embodied in the following platform:
We, the members of the San Jose Turn Verein, (Club) propose by our union to aid each other in rearing a people strong in both body and mind. We recognize in the dissemination of culture and the fostering of ethical and moral principles the only means of effecting a thorough reform of social, religious and political life. We strive for the development of the republic on a truly human republican basis. We, therefore, oppose most decidedly every attempt to interfere with the liberty of conscience, and also all legislative encroachments that are hostile to the perfection and developments of our free institutions.

Letter from Bundesprasident Waldheim

Der Bundespräsident

Wien, am 24. März 1988

Sehr geehrte Frau Brand!

Im Hinblick auf die Vielzahl der in den letzten Wochen eingegangenen Briefe, ist es mir nicht möglich, Ihr freundliches Schreiben im Einzelnen zu beantworten. Seien Sie aber versichert, daß ich Ihre Bekundung der Solidarität sehr geschätzt habe. Ich möchte Ihnen hiefür meinen aufrichtigen Dank zum Ausdruck bringen.

Mit allen guten Wünschen und den besten Grüßen

Ihr

[signature]

This is a response to my letter to President Waldheim of Austria and president of the UN after having been forbidden to visit the United States by the American government.

The letter says:

Because of the many letters I have received within the last couple of weeks, it is not possible for me to answer each letter in detail. Be assured that I have treasured your statement and solidarity with all my heart.

I like express my sincere thanks to you.

Best wishes and regards,
Kurt Waldheim

Letter from Dr. Philipp Jenninger

Dr. Philipp Jenninger
Präsident des Deutschen Bundestages a.D.

5300 Bonn, 9. März 1989
Bundeshaus

Frau
Maria Brand
1338 Elsona Drive

94087-Sunnyvale, California
USA

Sehr geehrte Frau Brand!

Leider komme ich erst jetzt dazu, Ihnen für Ihren freundlichen Brief, Ihre Anteilnahme und das Mitgefühl im Zusammenhang mit meiner Rede vom 10. November 1988 und meinem Rücktritt vom Amt des Bundestagspräsidenten zu danken.

In über 10.000 Zuschriften haben mir inzwischen viele Menschen aus dem In- und Ausland versichert, daß sie Sinn und Inhalt meiner Rede richtig verstanden haben. Das gibt mir die Kraft, mich auch weiterhin für die Wahrheit einzusetzen und meine politische Arbeit fortzusetzen.

Mit freundlichen Grüßen

In response to a letter I had written to Mr. Jenninger regarding a speech he had given on November 10, 1988, which most of the representatives of the Bundeshaus found offensive. Showing their displeasure, they walked out. The speech cost Mr. Jenninger his position as president of the House of Representatives in Bonn. I felt that Mr. Jenninger was right, and the protesters were hypocrites.

This is what Mr. Jenninger replied:

Dear Mrs. Brand

I am sorry I have not had time to respond and thank you for your friendly letter and compassion expressed in connection with the speech I gave and my withdrawal from my position as President of the Bundestag, on November 10, 1988, sooner.

Because of more than 10,000 letters from people in Germany as well as other countries I was assured that the context and meaning of my speech was correctly interpreted. That will give me the strength to continue my quest for the truth in my political work in the future.

With best regards,
Philipp Jenninger

Invitation from Vice President Dan Quayle

Vice President Dan Quayle

February 28, 1989

Maria Brand
1338 Elsona Drive
Sunnyvale, CA 94087

Dear Friend,

It gives me great pleasure to inform you that at the last membership meeting of the Republican Senatorial Inner Circle, your name was placed in nomination by Senator S. I. Hayakawa and you were accepted for membership.

To welcome you to the Inner Circle, Marilyn and I would like to personally invite you to the Vice President's residence on Monday, April 10th, for a private cocktail party during our upcoming Spring Briefing.

Our official business meetings open the morning of April 10th when you'll be participating in closed-door strategy sessions that will give you an insider's look at the Bush Administration's legislative gameplan and the 1990 Senate elections. You'll also be invited to take part in something truly unique to the Inner Circle. After a day of briefings you'll be the honored guest at a VIP dinner hosted by a Republican Senator, Cabinet member or Administration official.

Distinguished Americans who have already joined the Inner Circle include Bob Hope, Arnold Schwarzenegger, Stephanie Zimbalist, George Shultz and Mario Andretti. Not all of our members are this well known. But like you, every one of them has demonstrated a truly exemplary commitment to our nation's ideals and principles.

My close friend, former Senate Majority Leader Howard Baker, will be mailing your formal invitation to join the Inner Circle in a few days. I urge you to respond as soon as possible.

I look forward to meeting you on April 10th!

Sincerely,

Dan Quayle
Vice President

REPUBLICAN SENATORIAL INNER CIRCLE • 425 SECOND STREET, N.E. • WASHINGTON, D.C. 20002
PAID FOR AND AUTHORIZED BY THE NATIONAL REPUBLICAN SENATORIAL COMMITTEE.
CONTRIBUTIONS TO THE NATIONAL REPUBLICAN SENATORIAL COMMITTEE ARE NOT TAX DEDUCTIBLE AS CHARITABLE CONTRIBUTIONS
FOR FEDERAL INCOME TAX PURPOSES. NOT PRINTED AT GOVERNMENT EXPENSE.

Mr. Dan Quayle served as the forty-fourth vice president of the United States under President G. H. Bush. I have never been a member of the Republican Party. I did not respond to this letter.

Friendship Award presented by the German government

The German government honored me with the Friendship Award, which I shared with my husband, Walter. Without his support I would not have been able to spend the time, money, and energy to keep working on the "German American Heritage" project for all these years.

I thank him with all my heart.

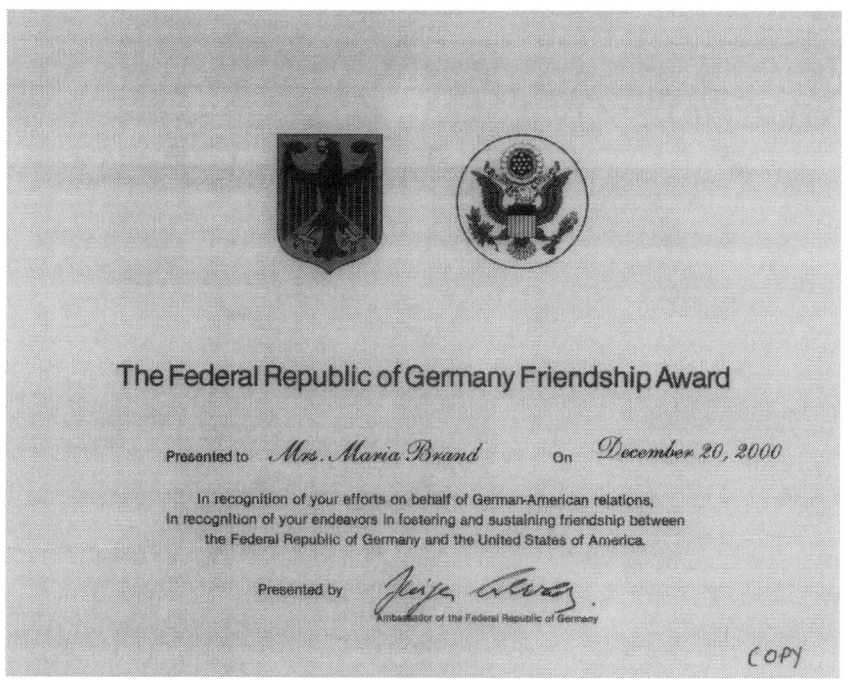

This award was presented to us at the Pacific Saengerbund festival at the Elks Club in San Jose, California

UGAC, Inc.
UNITED GERMAN-AMERICAN COMMITTEE
OF THE USA, INC.

Bern E. Deichmann – President, Volker Schmeissner – 1st Vice President
Bernhard Keppler – 2nd Vice President, Erich Ast – Secretary/Treasurer
Frederick Hansen – Recording Secretary

Inviting you to our Annual

German Heritage Festival

Honoring : **Mr. & Mrs. Walter & Maria Brand, San Jose, CA**

Recipient of this years award for the most "Distinguished German-American" for their untiring work on behalf of the German Cause.

Please join us at our UGAC Annual Council of 1000 Banquet
(black tie optional)
at the Phoenix Club in Anaheim, California
1340 S. Sanderson Avenue
on Sunday 3:30 pm, November 16, 2003

to honor *Mr. & Mrs. Walter & Maria Brand*, as well as all new Council of the 1000 members,
and at the same time enjoy an exciting and elegant cultural program, dining and dancing included.

$100.00 per Person

For information and reservation call 760-726-6184

Seating is limited and only by reservation.

Famous TV Star Eric Braeden will be our Main Speaker

(you see him on CBS/ The Young and the Restless)

Support UGAC-- on the road to establish a National Heritage Site in Washington, D.C. for all Americans of German decent, honoring their many contributions to the development of the United States of America.

UGAC Washington DC Headquarter. P.O. Box 279, Waldorf, MD 20604
1-866-868-8422 (toll free) regular Phone: 202-467-5000 • Fax: 202-467-5440 •
E-mail: ugac@aol.com   home page: www.ugac.org

Distinguished German-American Award

**2003
Distinguished German–Americans
of the Year Award**

presented to

Walter & Maria Brand

in honor of their exceptional contributions to the German-American community over the past decades and for their continuous and positive encouragement of German-American relations in the USA and abroad

by

The United German-American Committee of the USA, Inc.
at the Council of 1000 Banquet, Anaheim, CA – USA

Bern E. Deichmann
President

November 16, 2003

This was a festive occasion. We both felt honored but also deserving. This award is presented once a year. The celebration took place at the Phoenix Club in Los Angeles.

The San Francisco Bay Area guests came by bus; participants from the East Coast and Midwest flew in for the occasion. Much work and effort had gone into the preparation. The choir sang, the speeches were full of enthusiasm for our German heritage, and everyone expressed the urgency for establishing a museum in Washington, DC. The food was delicious, and the band played for our dancing pleasure. It was indeed a very memorable day for all of us.

Acceptance speech by Maria Brand

(After receiving the award, November, 16, 2003)

My husband and I like to thank the United German American Committee, UGAC USA for presenting us with this prestigious award.

Every person who contributes his talent, time and energy to keep the German American Societies alive and well, shares in this award. This is for the people who promote and work at festivals; take a position as a board member of a Verein; organize a coffee klatch, singing event, Schuetzenfest or whatever else the occasion calls for, is deserving of recognition.

A special "Thank you" to Mr. and Mrs. Galleisky and their volunteers for making this fundraiser possible.

We hope that the German American Museum, in Washington D.C. becomes a reality, for it will reflect the values the immigrants from the heart of Europe brought to these shores. If we look about us, we can still see the products of their dreams, skills, talents and work ethics.

The old values have proven to be an asset to the immigrant for more than 400 years. They were his source of strength and comfort; they sustained his body and nurtured his soul. He applied the discipline he was taught in the old country to achieve goals, often greater than he had ever imagined.

A track record like this is hard to beat. We ought to do our best to preserve this roadmap not only for the German American descendents, but, for everyone who finds the pattern useful.

Let us combine all our efforts; let us build this German American National Museum for the purpose of sharing with our fellow citizens the role the German-speaking peoples played in the struggles and triumphs of this great nation, which is after all our chosen Heimat. The immigrants, who preceded us, have done their share, now it is our turn.

Let us not disappoint our descendents. Besides I can think of no better way to honor our new as well as our old homeland. Let us build the German American Museum in Washington DC.

Sincerely
Maria Brand

Recipients of the Distinguished German American of the Year Award

----

1987 – Karl Ehmer – New York

1988 – The Honorable Ruth E. Denk – New York

1989 – Werner Fricker – Pennsylvania

1990 – Eric Braeden – California

1991 – Albrecht Maier – New Jersey

1992 – Heinz C. Prechter – Michigan

1993 – Dr. George J. Beichl – Pennsylvania

1994 – Doris Meissner – Wisconsin

1995 – The honorable William Hetzler- New York

1996 – Bruno Karnas – Pennsylvania

1997 –.Gerald Kainz – Washington, D.C.

1998 – Professor Dr. Otto I. Walter, Esq. – New York

1999 – C. John Muller – Pennsylvania

2000 – John Patrick Schmitz, Esq. – Washington, D.C.

2001 – Detlef "Ted" Hierl – New Jersey

2002 – Dr. Don Heinrich Tolzmann – Ohio
2003 – Walter & Maria Brand – California
2004 – Al Wurz - Pennsylvania
2005 – Dr. Guenter Blobel – New York
2006 - General and Mrs, Schwarzkopf – Virginia
2007 – Margrit B. Krewson – Washington D.C.
2008 – Wilma L. Schmidt – New Jersey
2008 – Dr. Jesco von Puttkamer – Washington, D.C.
2009 – William R. Timken, Jr.

(It might be fun for you to goggle the people mentioned above.)

I'd like to finish my biography with an old German song known to almost everyone of my generation. In its original form it is a passive song. I have changed the text to make it into an active song.

Here it is:
Die Gedanken sind frei, man sollte sie wecken,
Um Geist und Verstand und die Gemueter zu strecken.
Kein Mensch soll uns wehren um diese zu naehren,
Es bleibet dabei, gruendlich denken macht frei.

Jeder denkt was er will, nicht nur was begluecked,
Wenn allein in der Still, es manchmal bedruecket.
Zusammen reden and regen, alle Hebel bewegen,
Es bleibet dabei, nach denken, handeln macht frei.

Best wishes to all of you
Sincerely,
Maria Brand